I0409708

Cubist Art Unleashed

Merging Reality and Imagination

ISBN: 9798853238190

Welcome to the exhilarating world of "Cubist Art Unleashed: Merging Reality and Imagination" In this captivating mindfulness coloring book, we embark on a voyage that defies conventional artistic boundaries and plunges headfirst into the realm of abstract shapes, fragmented perspectives, and a harmonious chaos of colors.

This book celebrates the avant-garde movement that emerged at the dawn of the 20th century - Cubism. A movement that ignited a creative revolution, transforming the way we perceive and interpret the world around us. Here, we venture beyond traditional art, as the visionaries of Cubism dared to merge reality and imagination, transcending the confines of time and space. Cubism beckons us to look beyond the surface, to delve into the intricacies of existence, and to embrace the beauty in the seemingly mundane.

This mindfulness coloring book is an invitation to immerse yourself in a dynamic world where imagination knows no bounds. It encourages you to question, to contemplate, and to unleash your own creative spirit. So, get ready to witness art unleashed! Let us journey together into the realm of Cubist marvels, where reality and imagination intertwine in an extraordinary dance of shapes and colors.

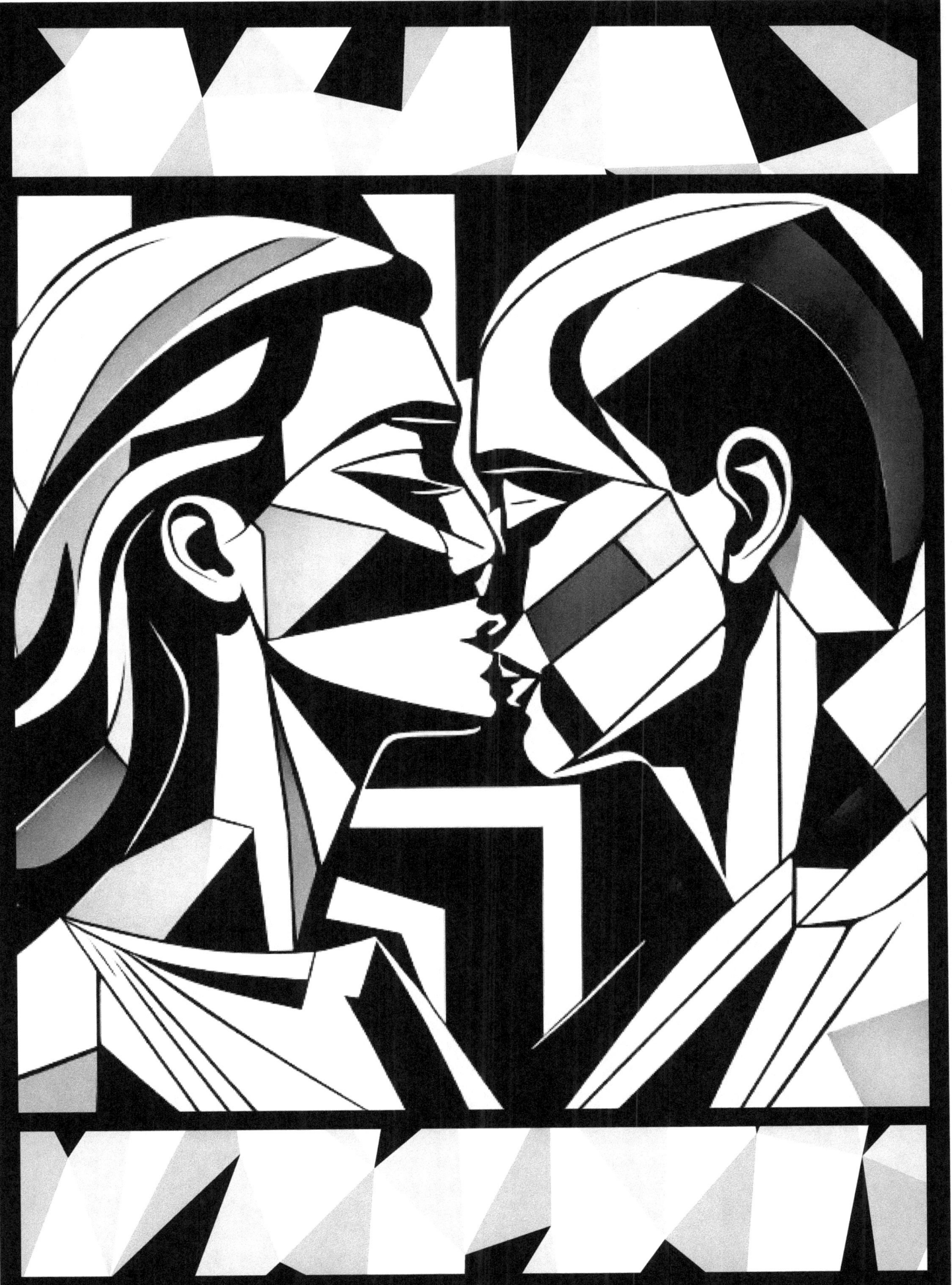

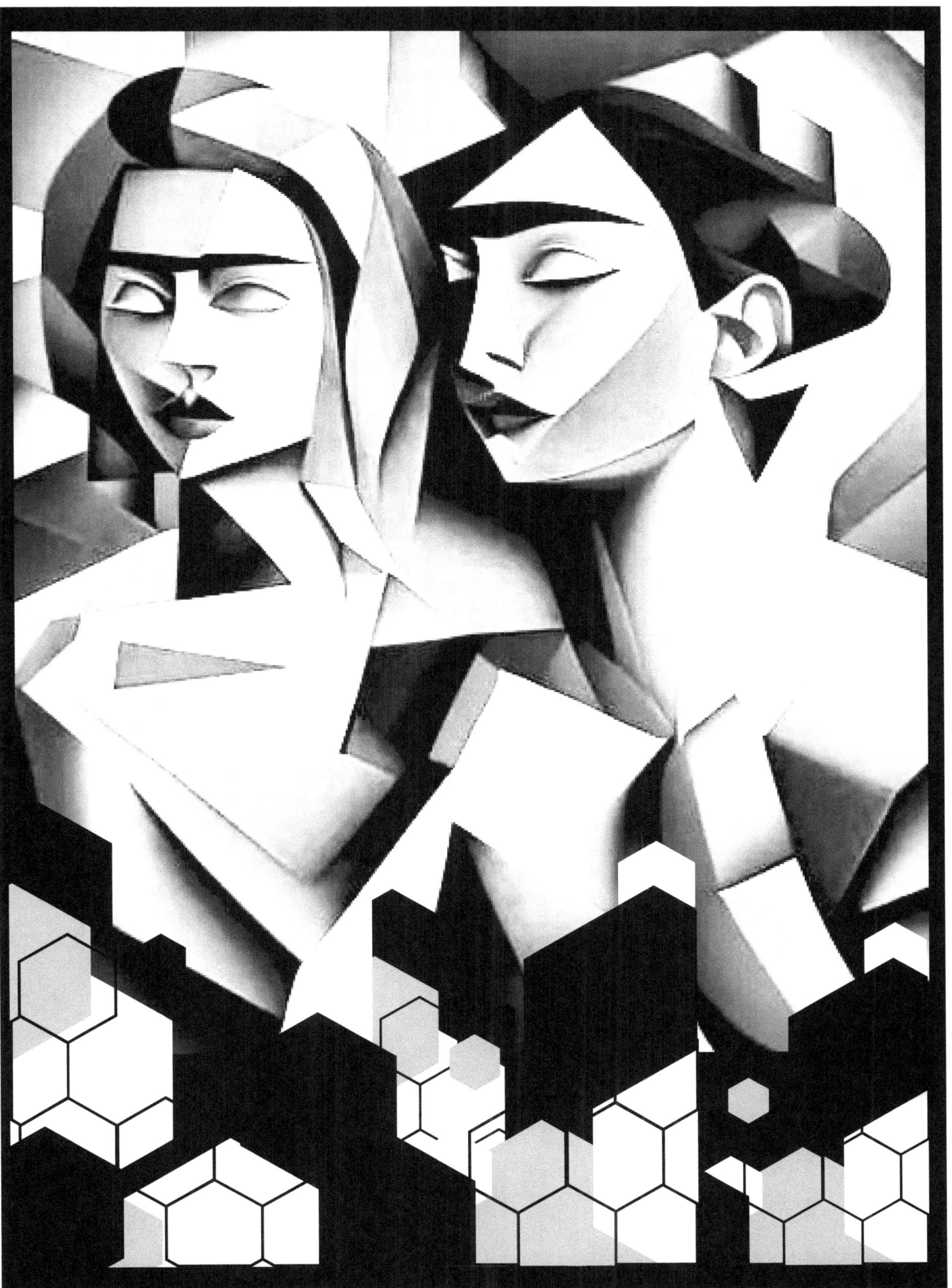

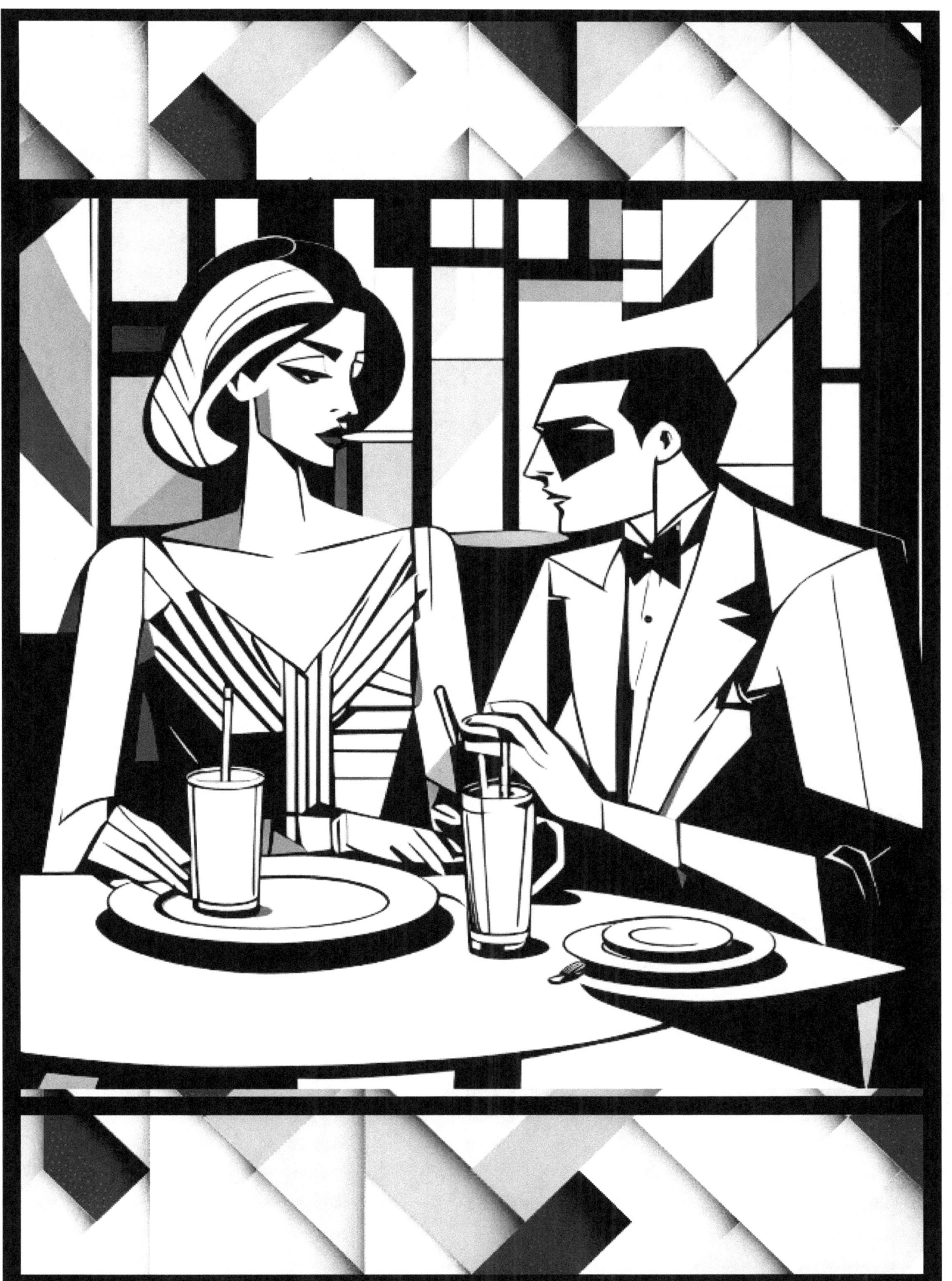

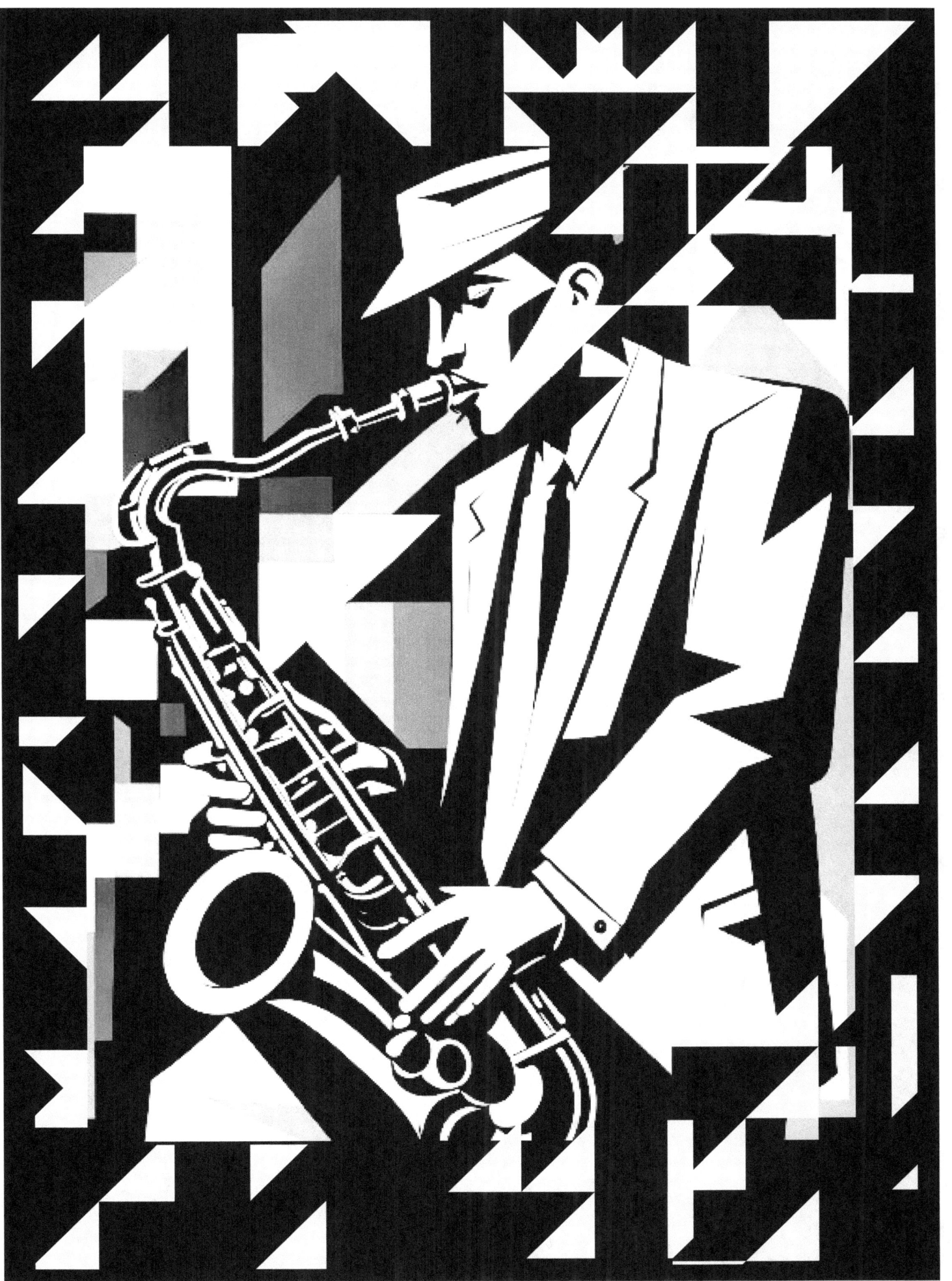

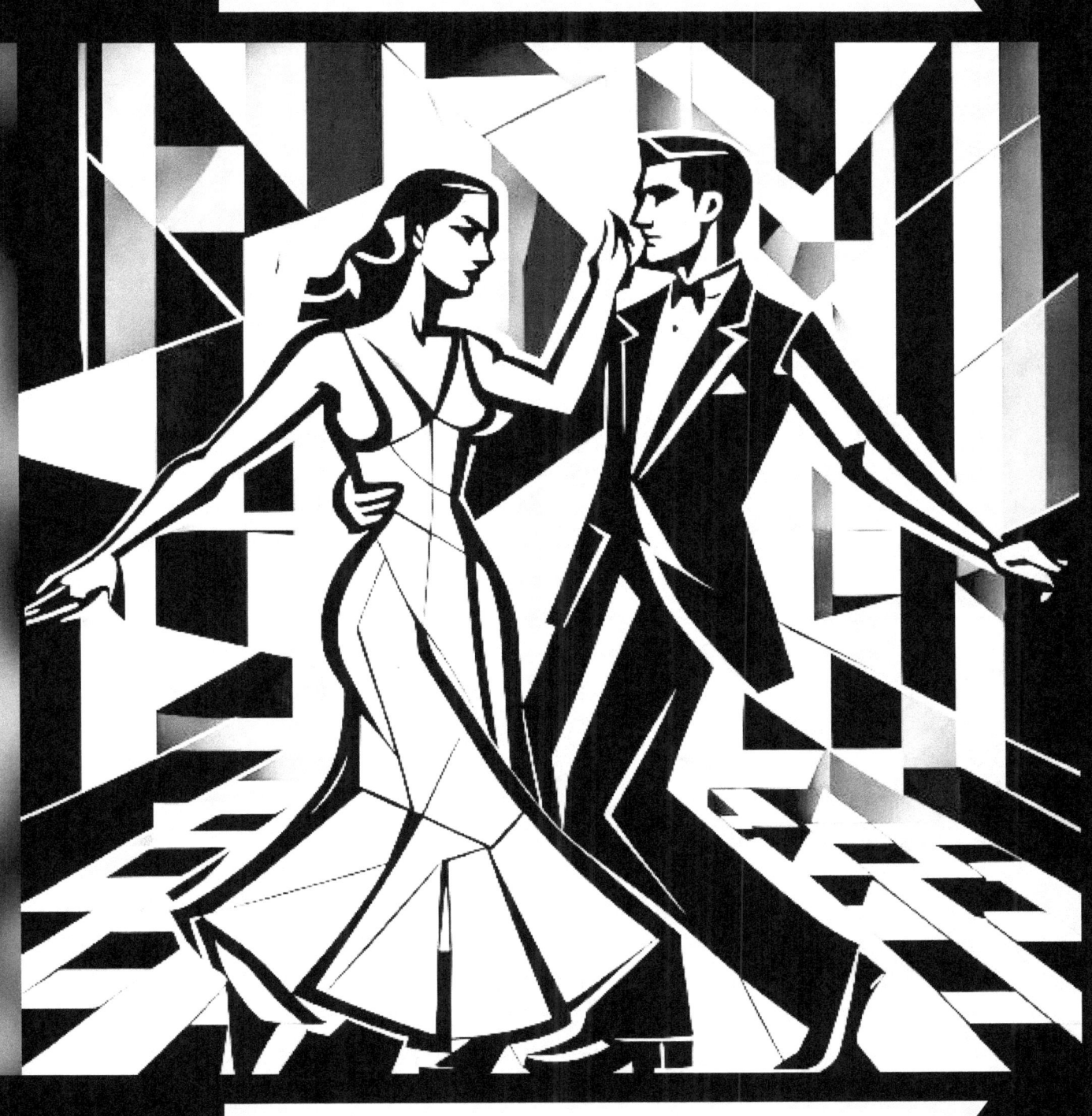

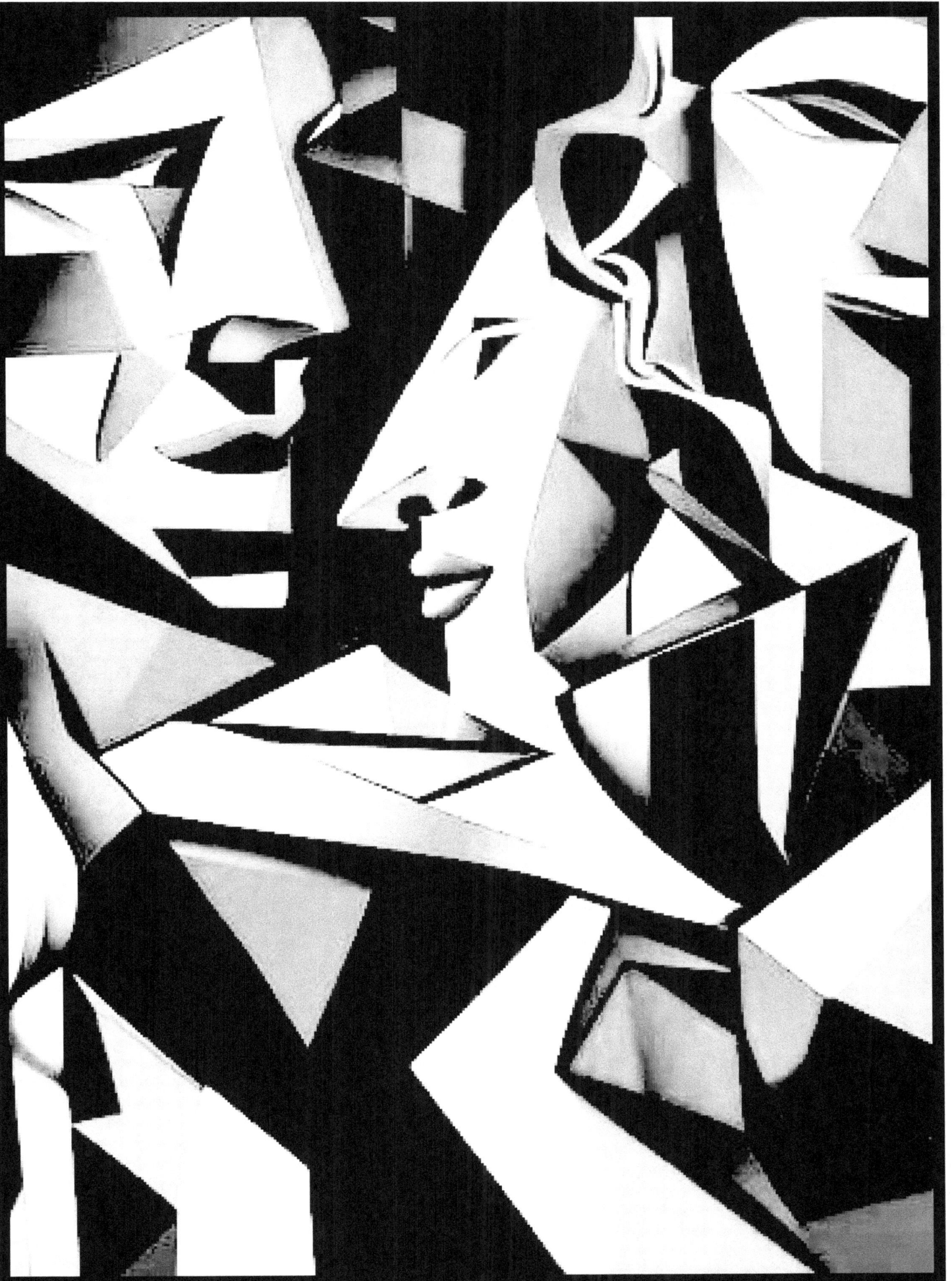

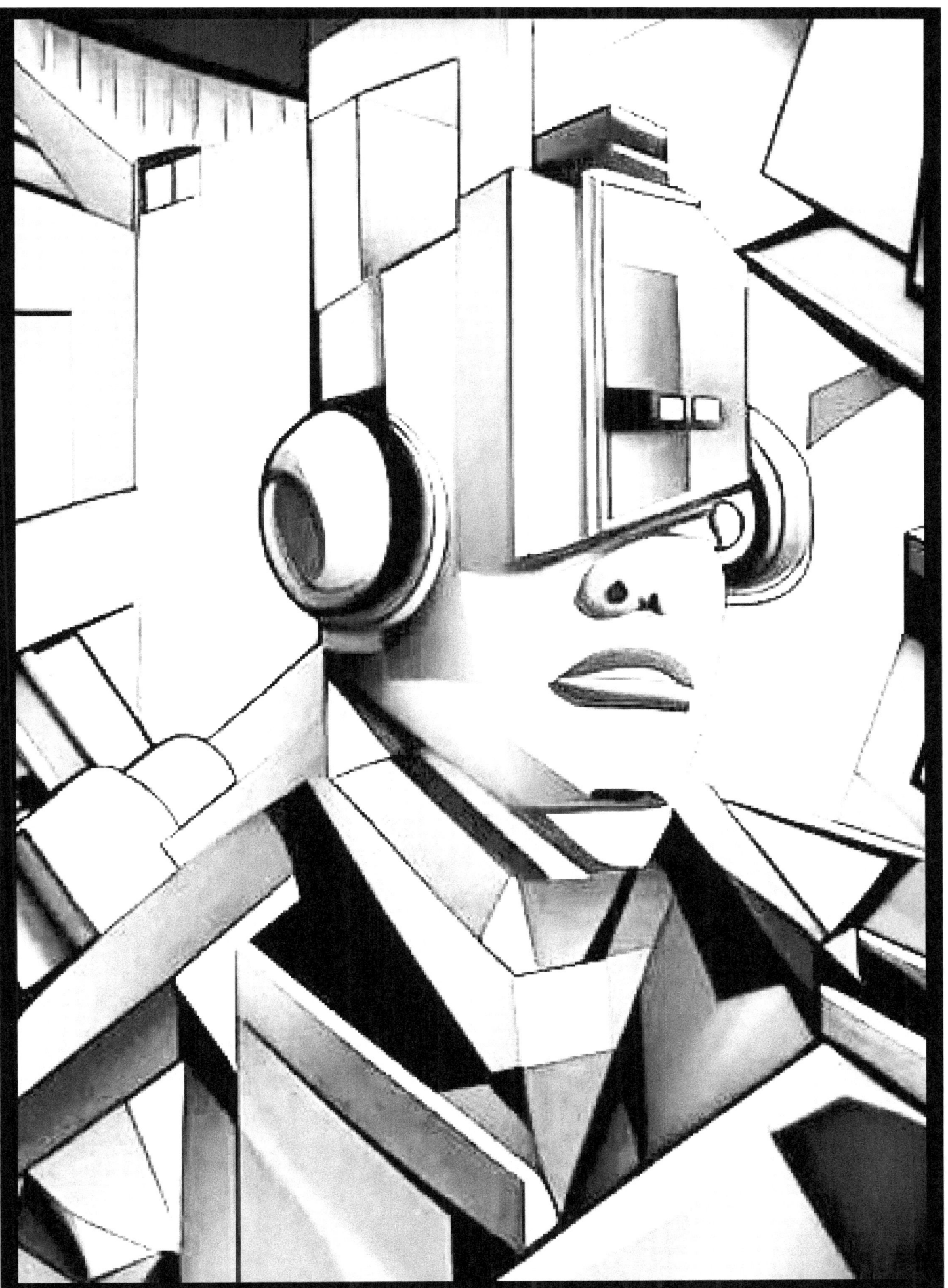

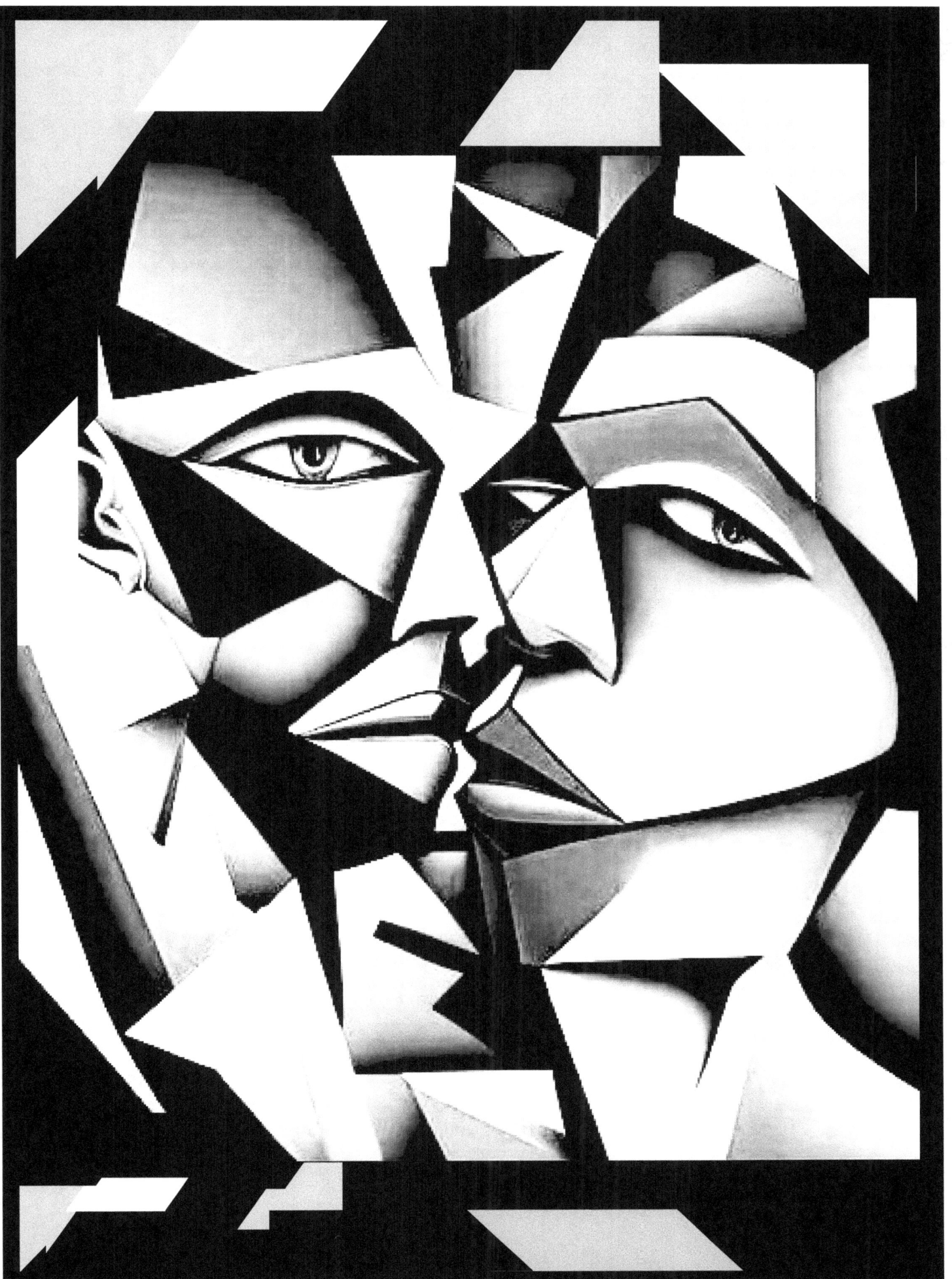

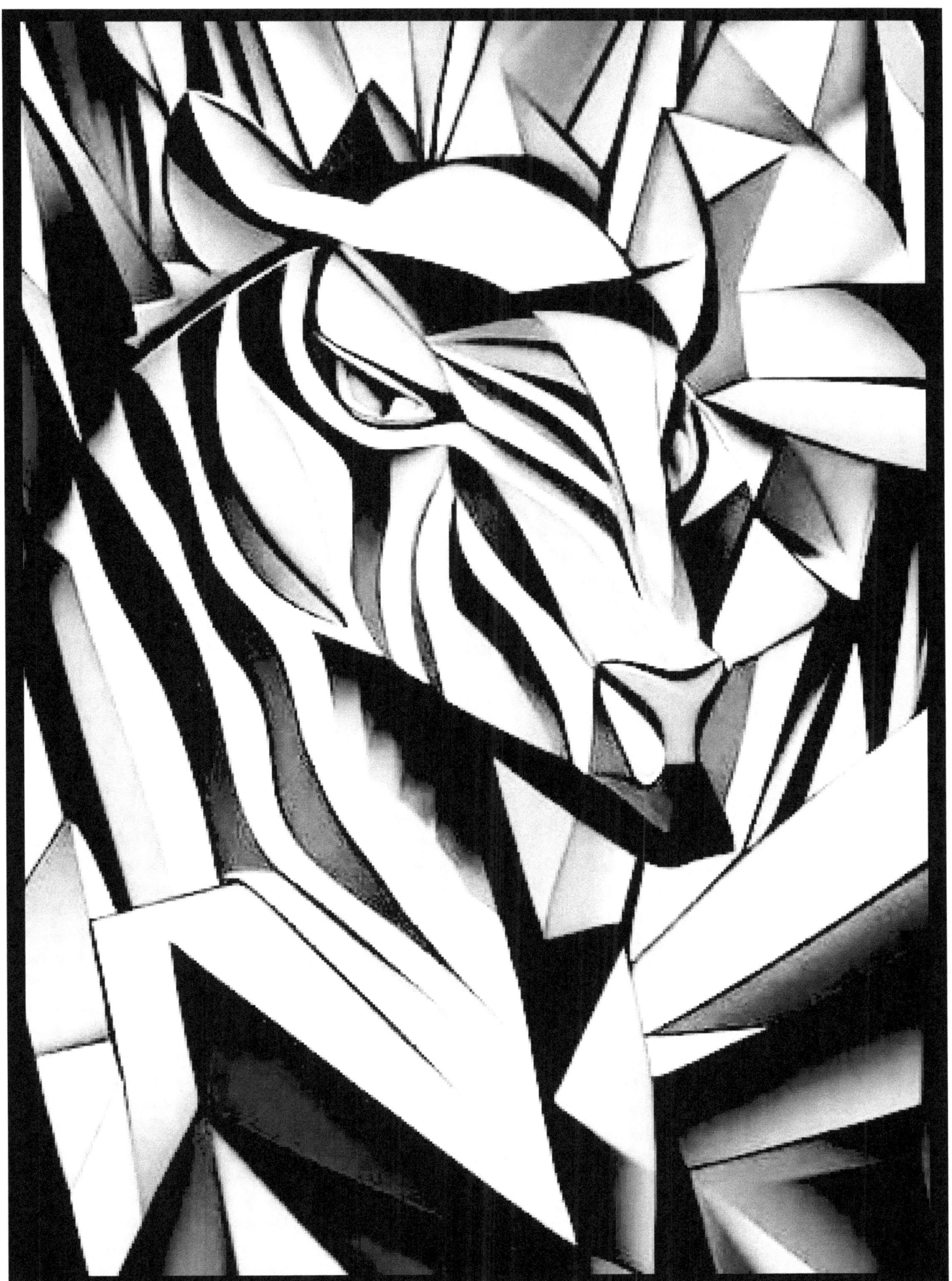

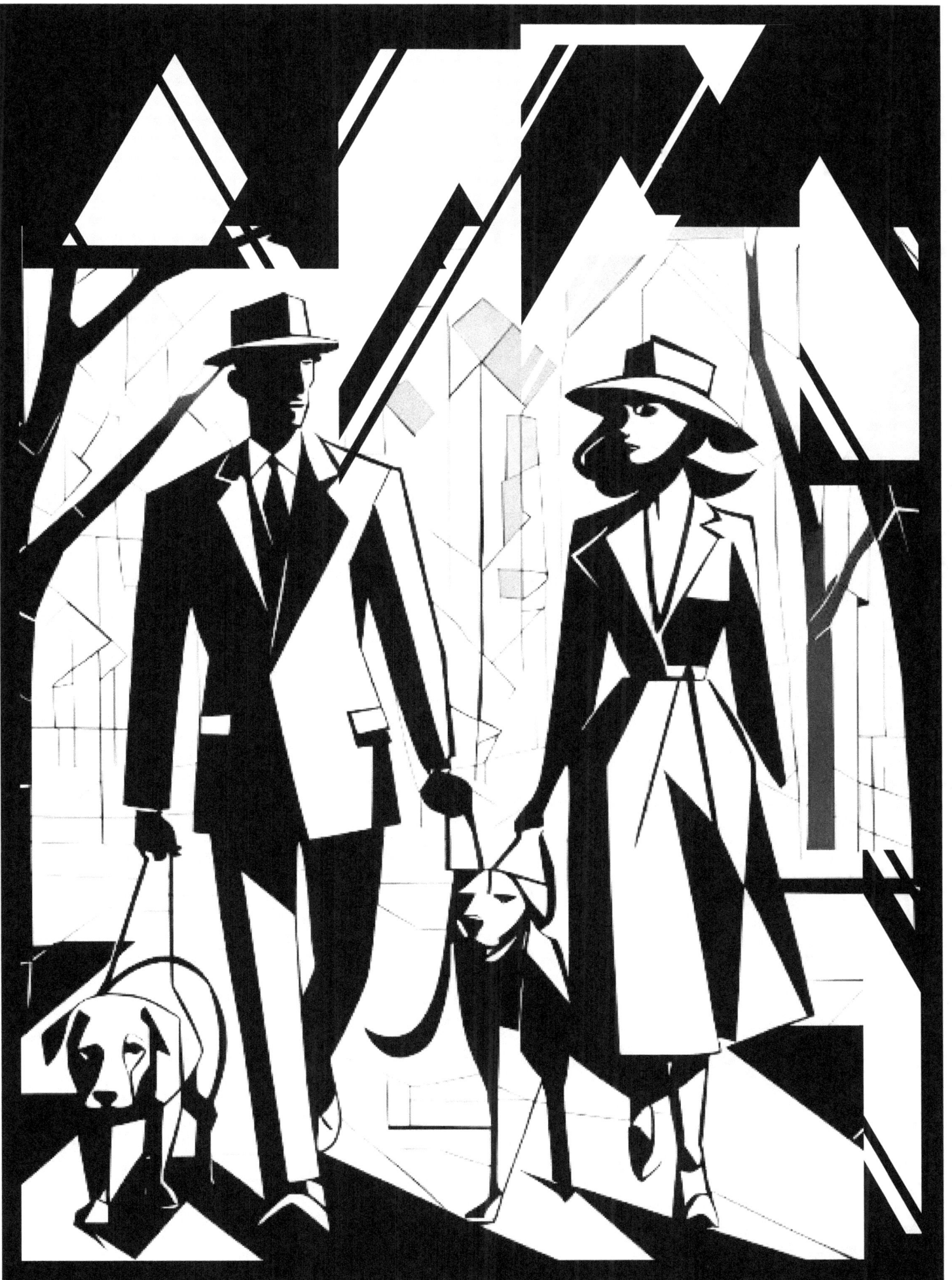

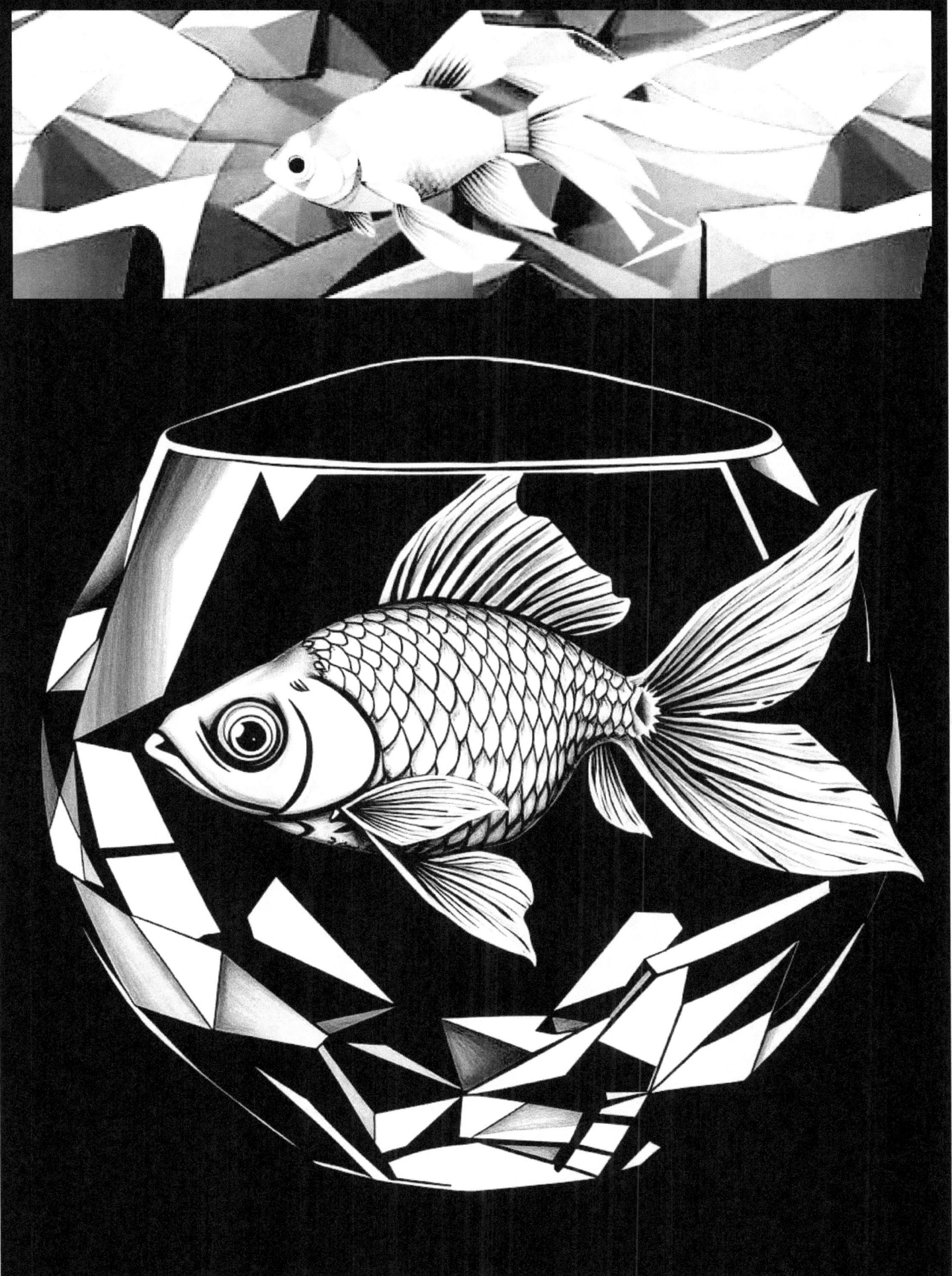

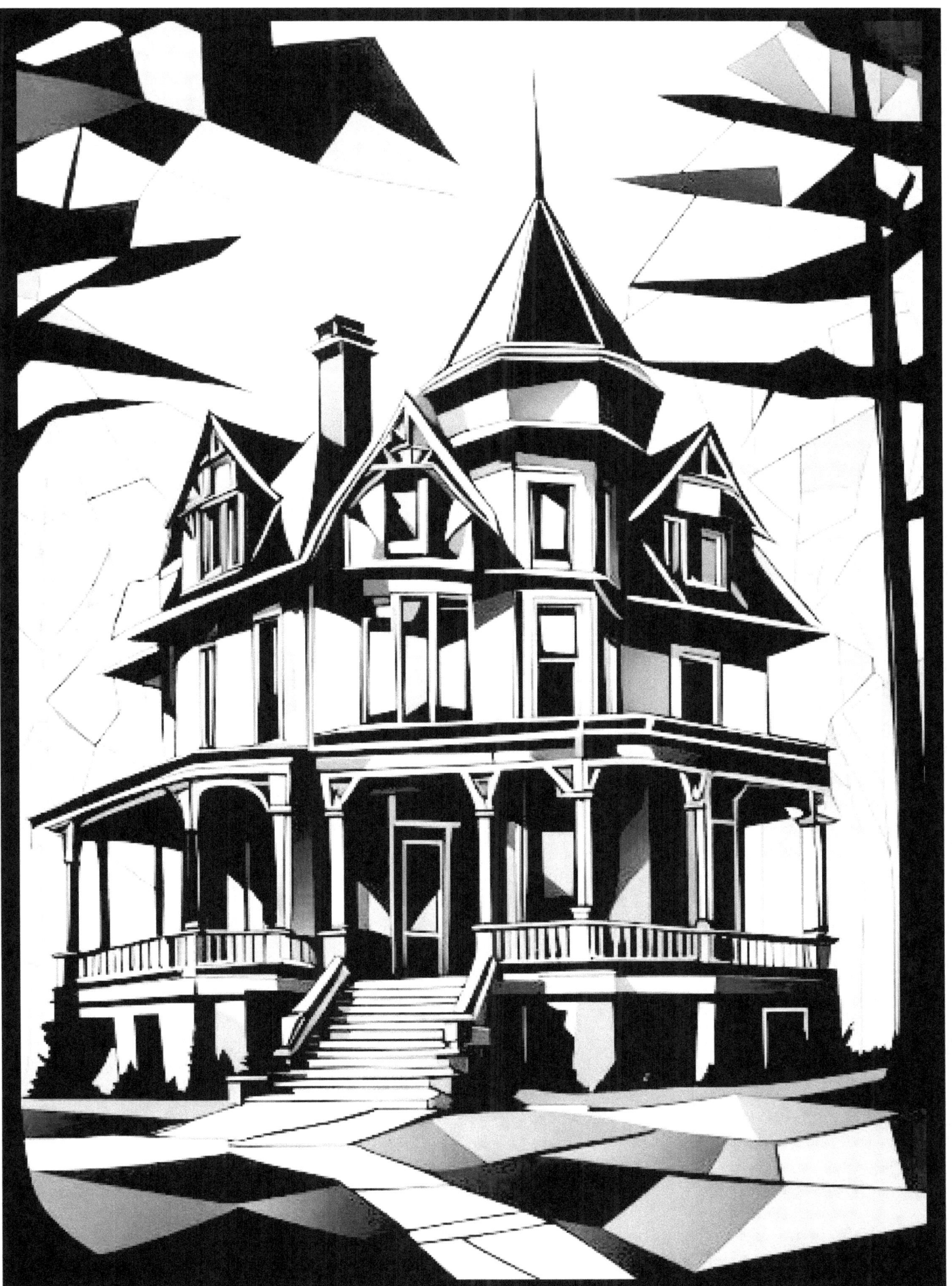

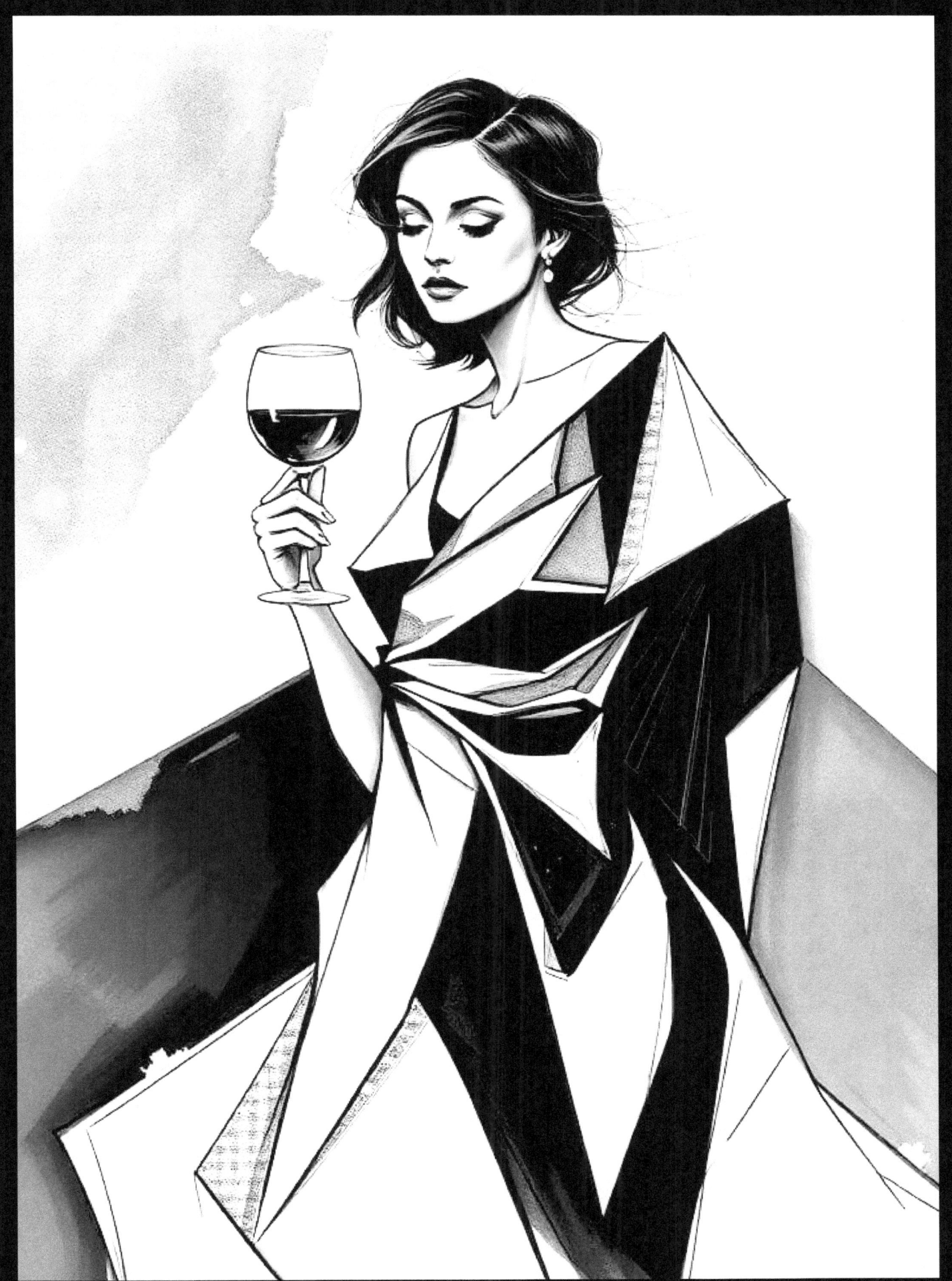

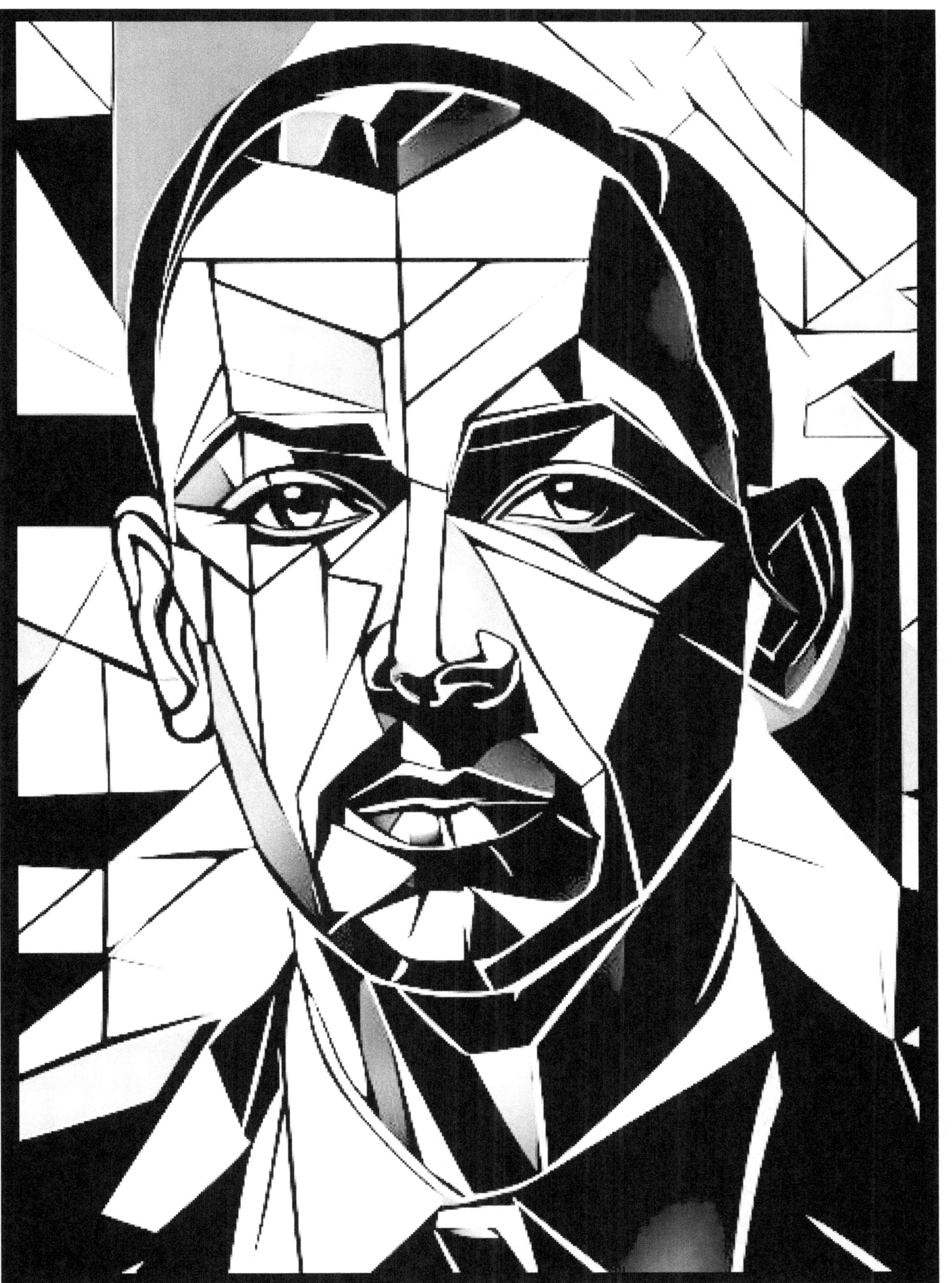

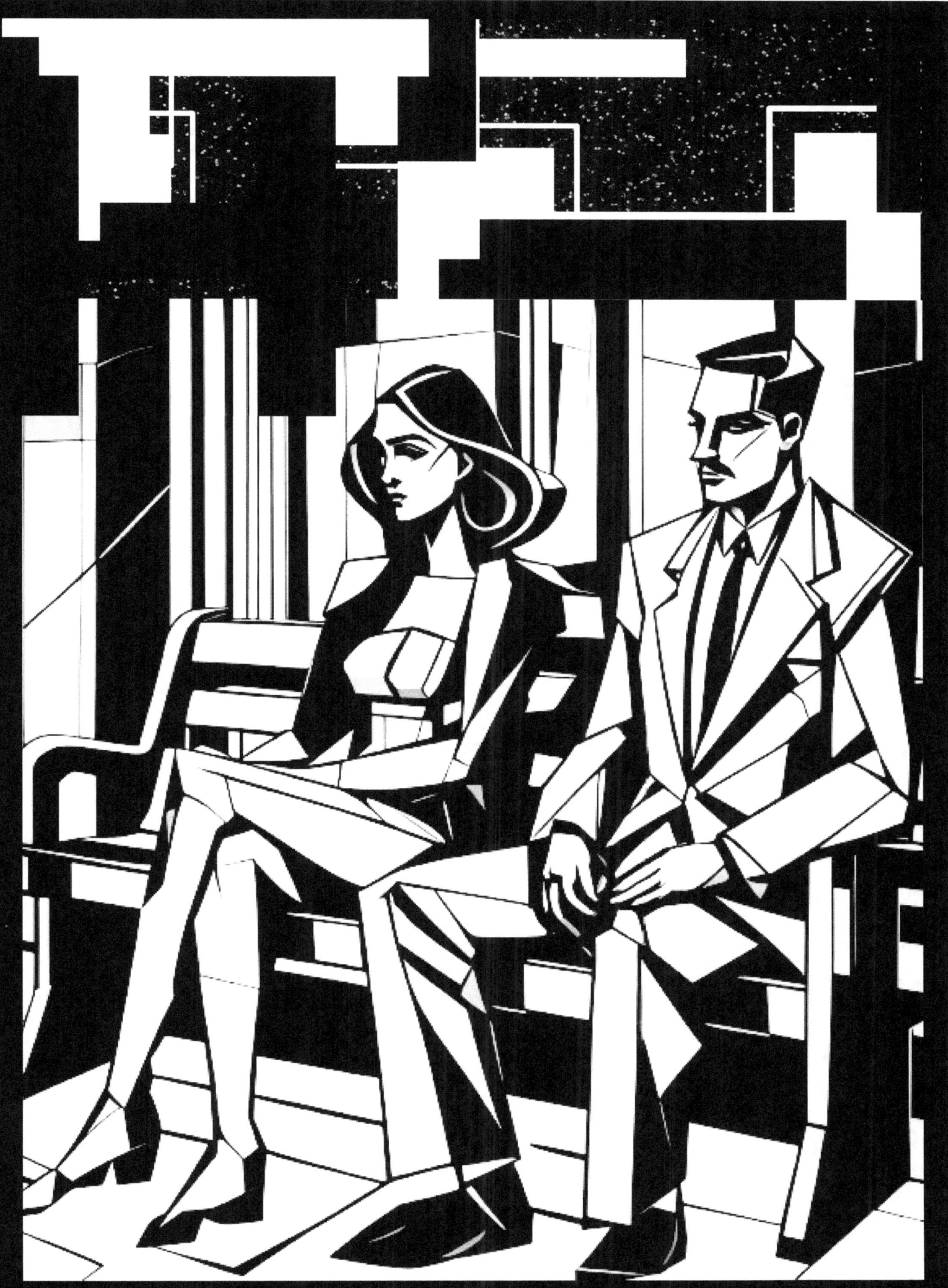

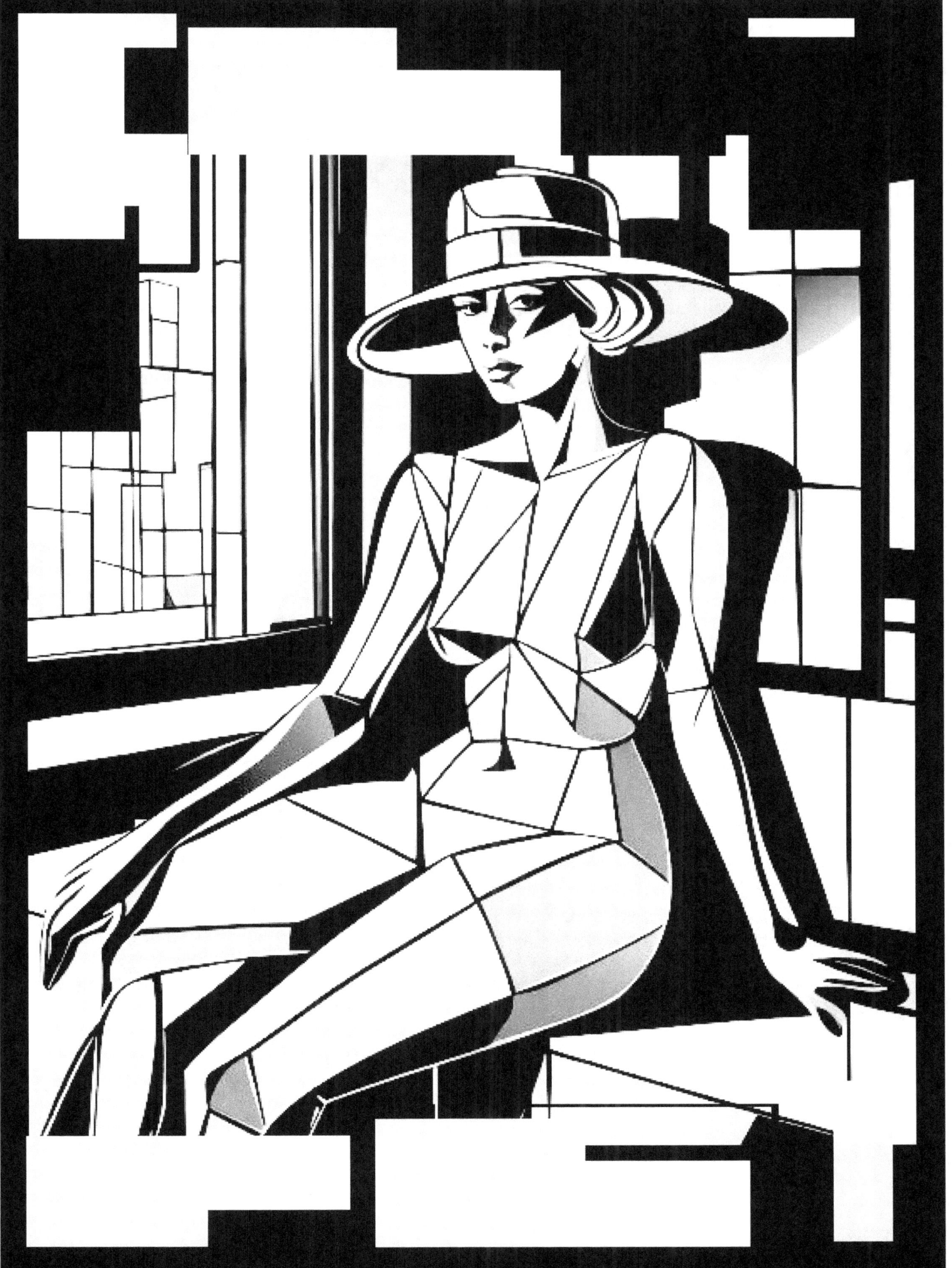

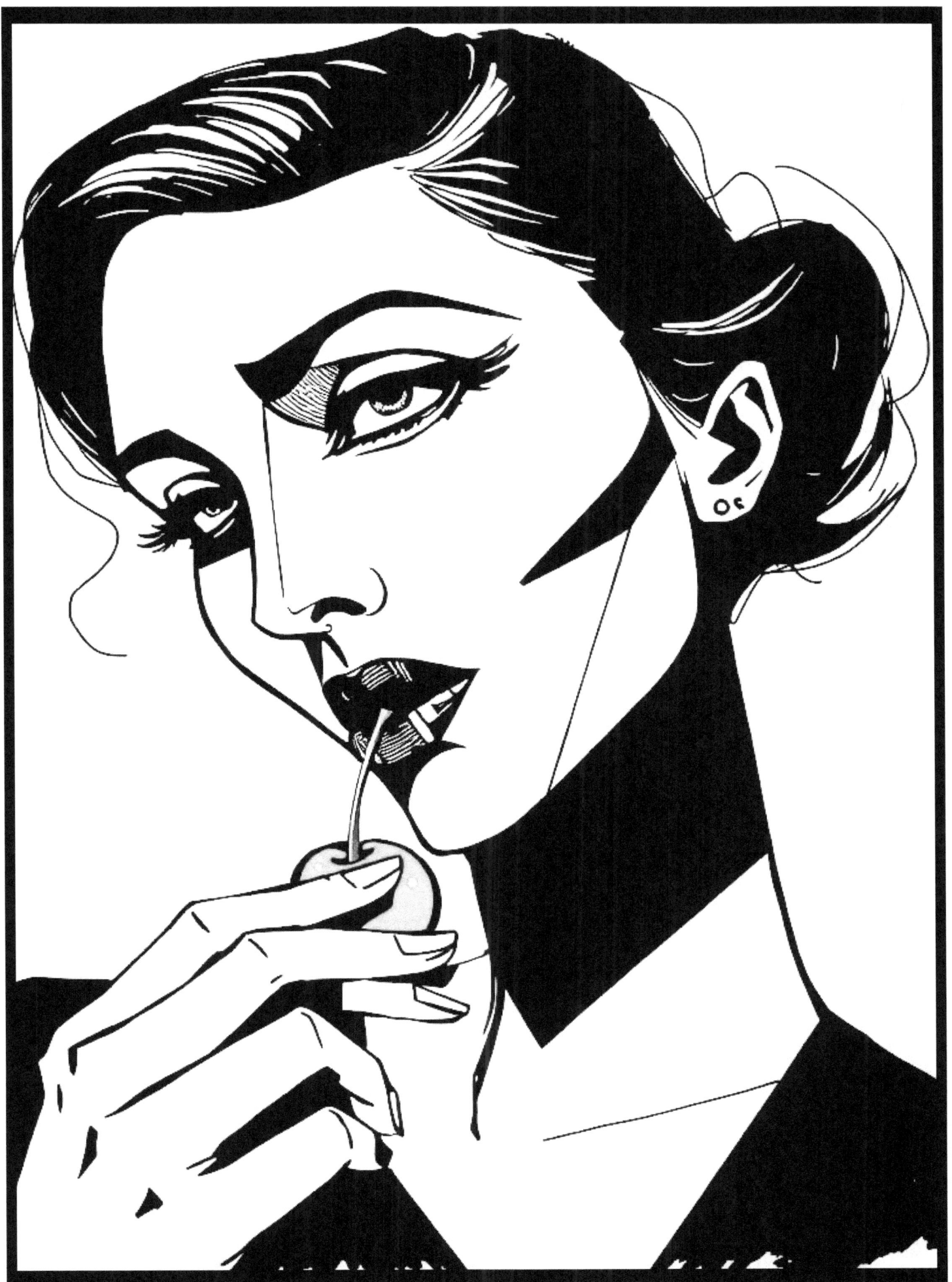

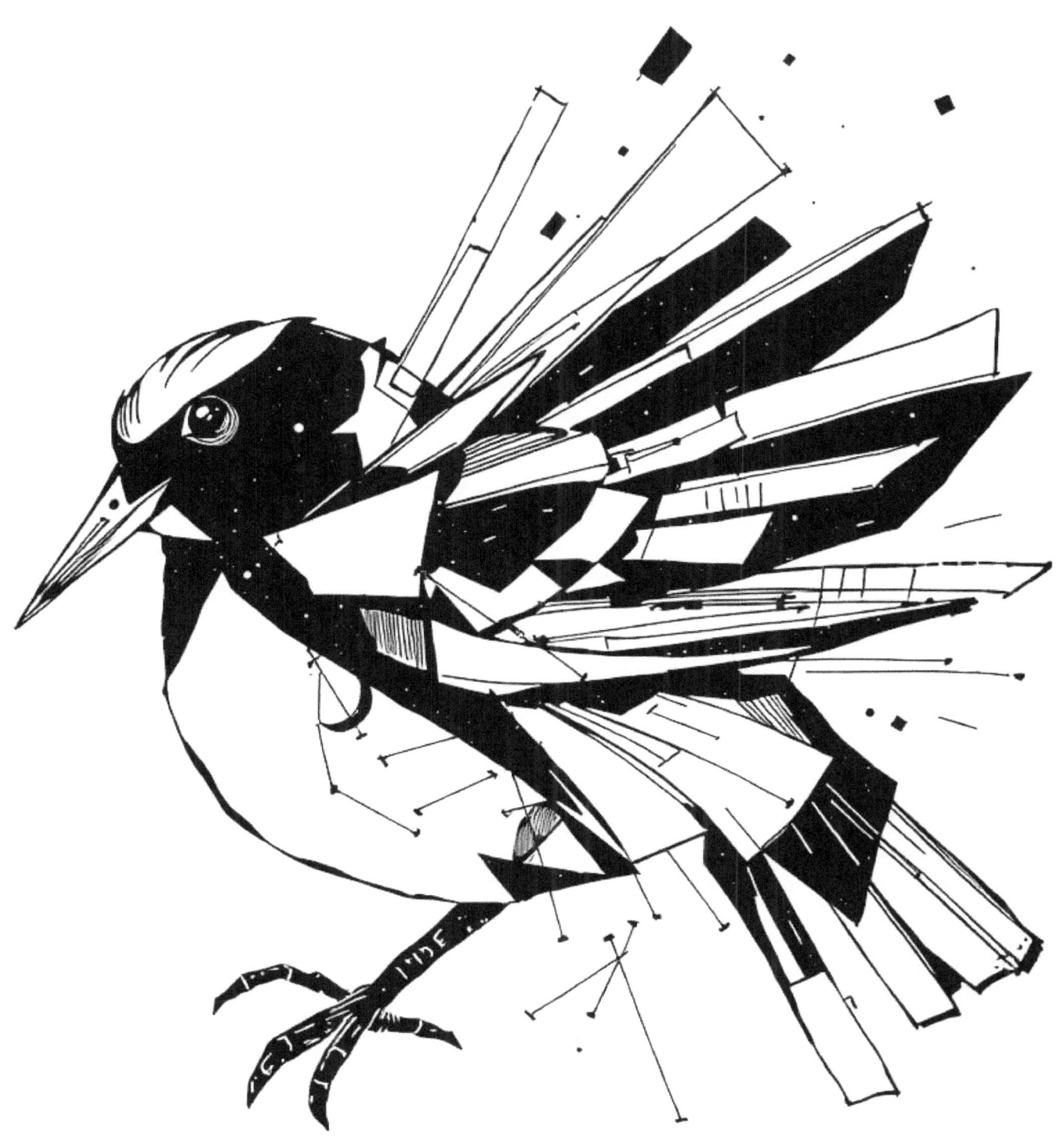

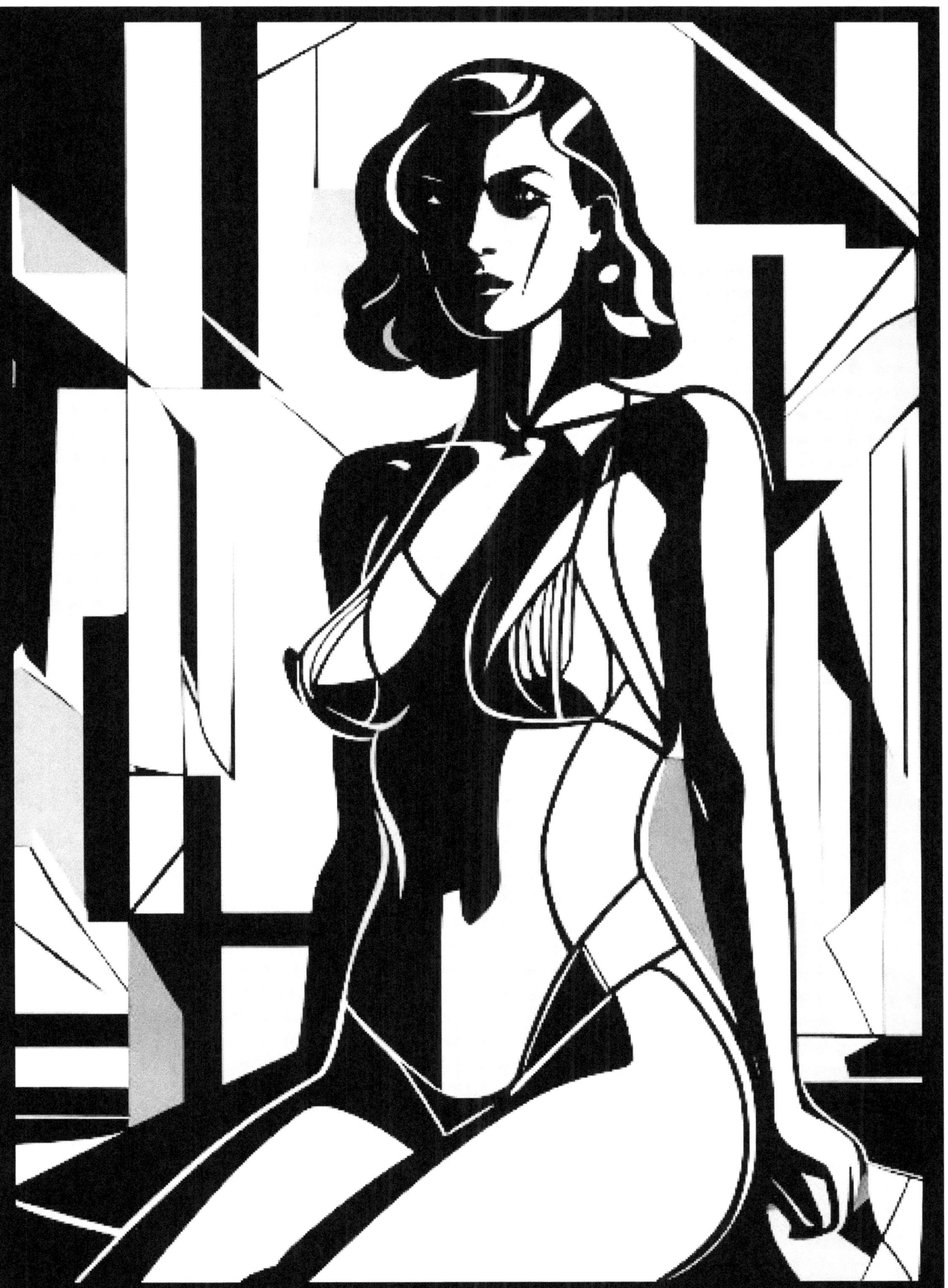

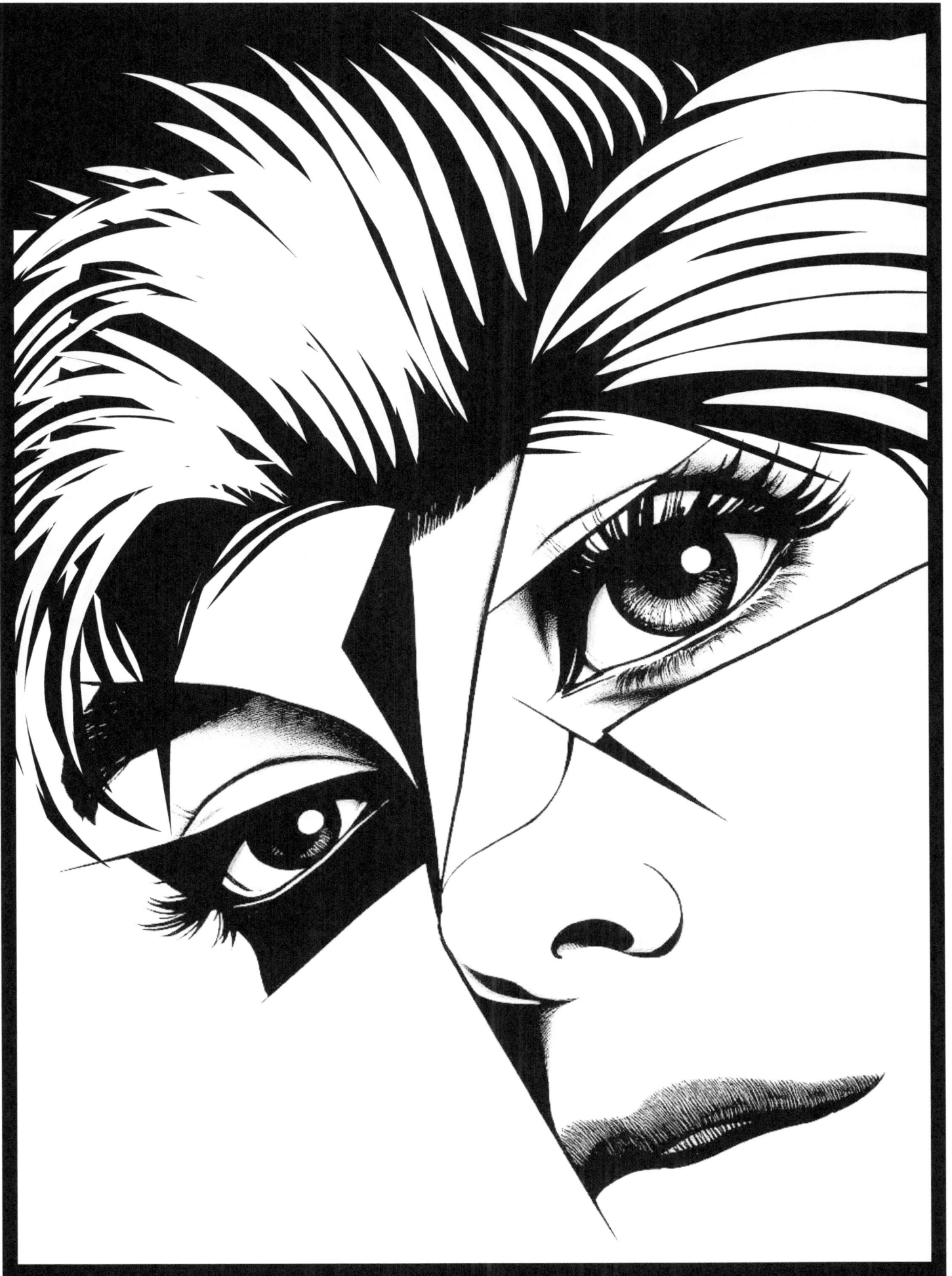

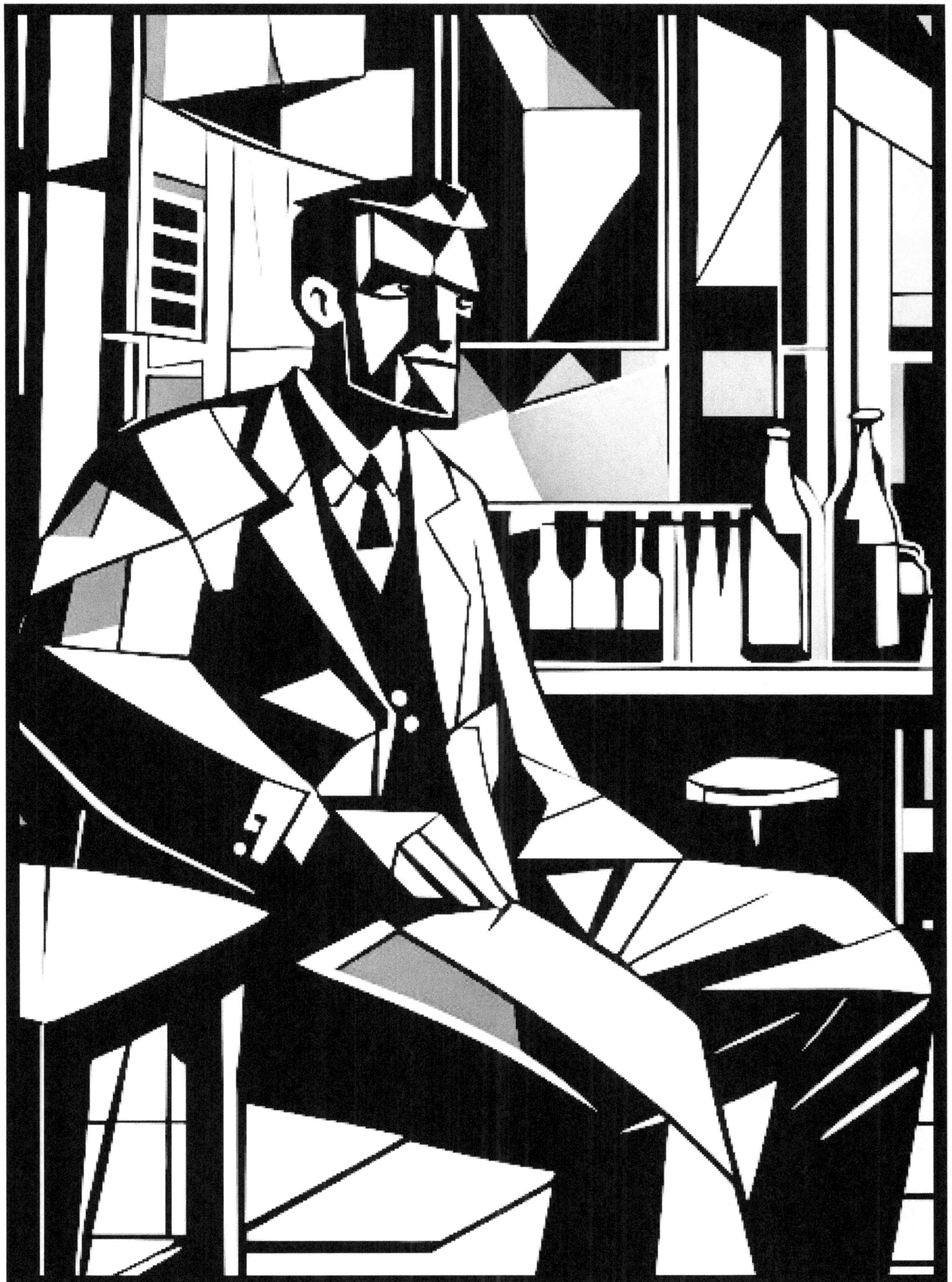

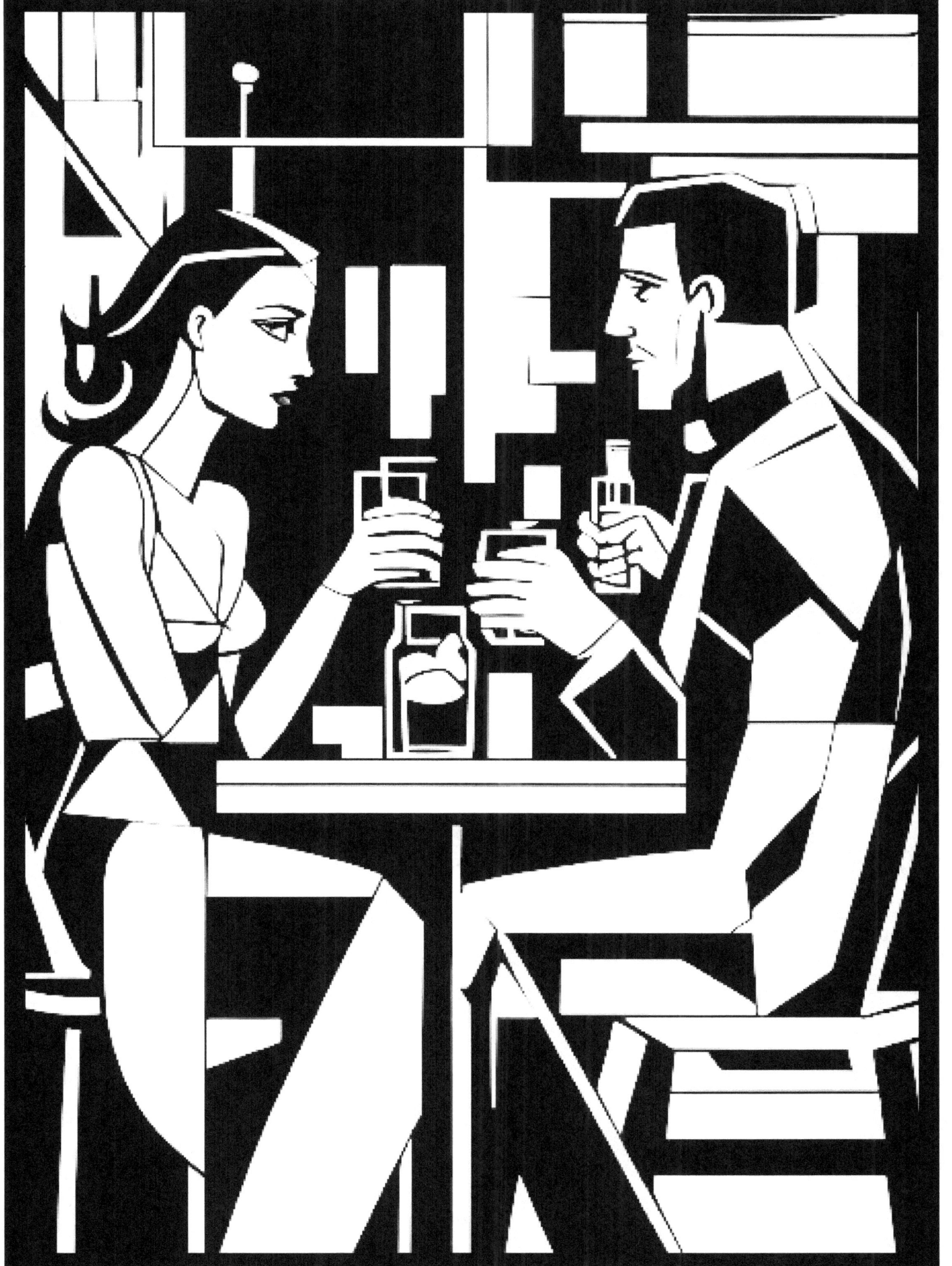

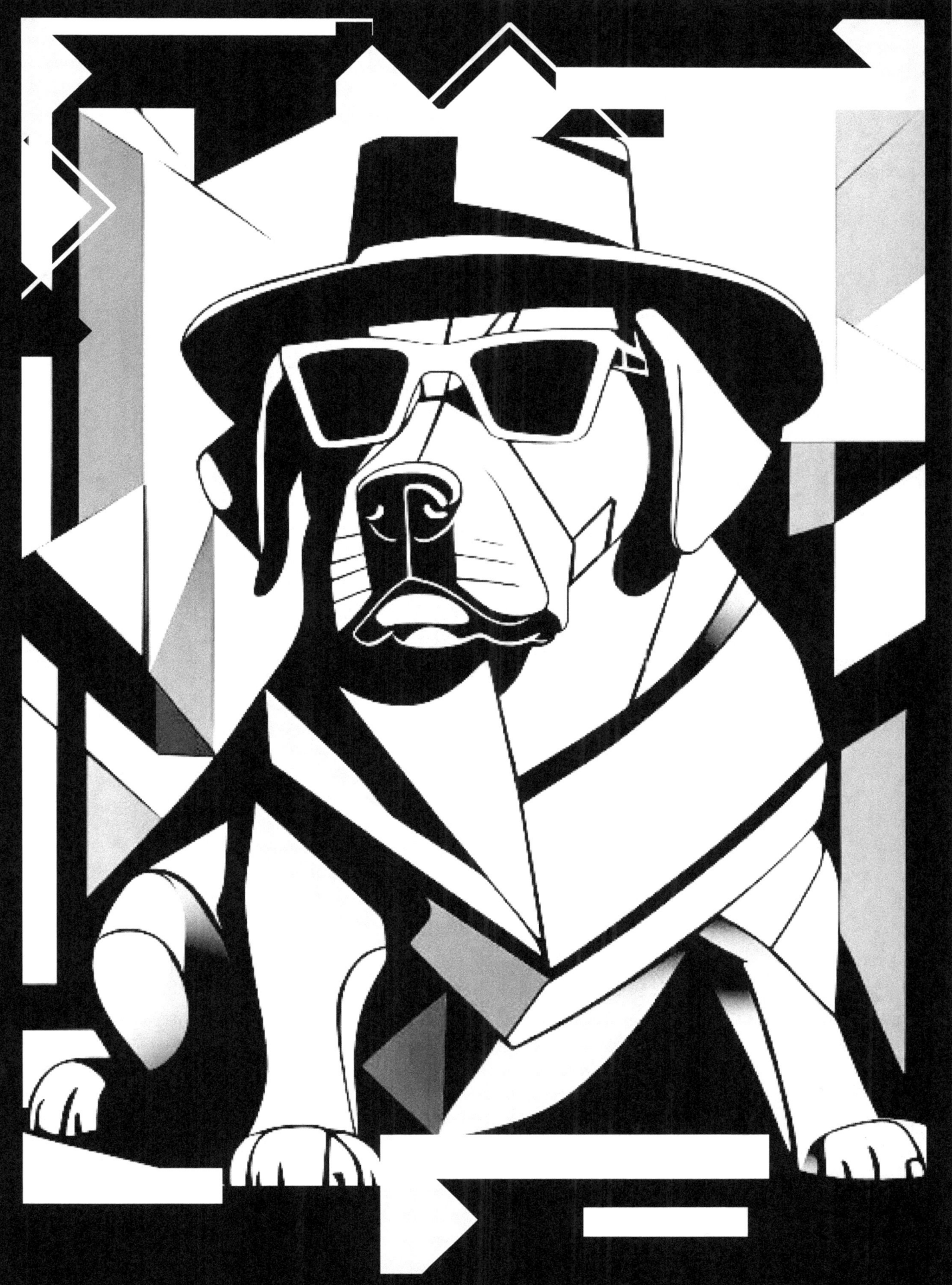

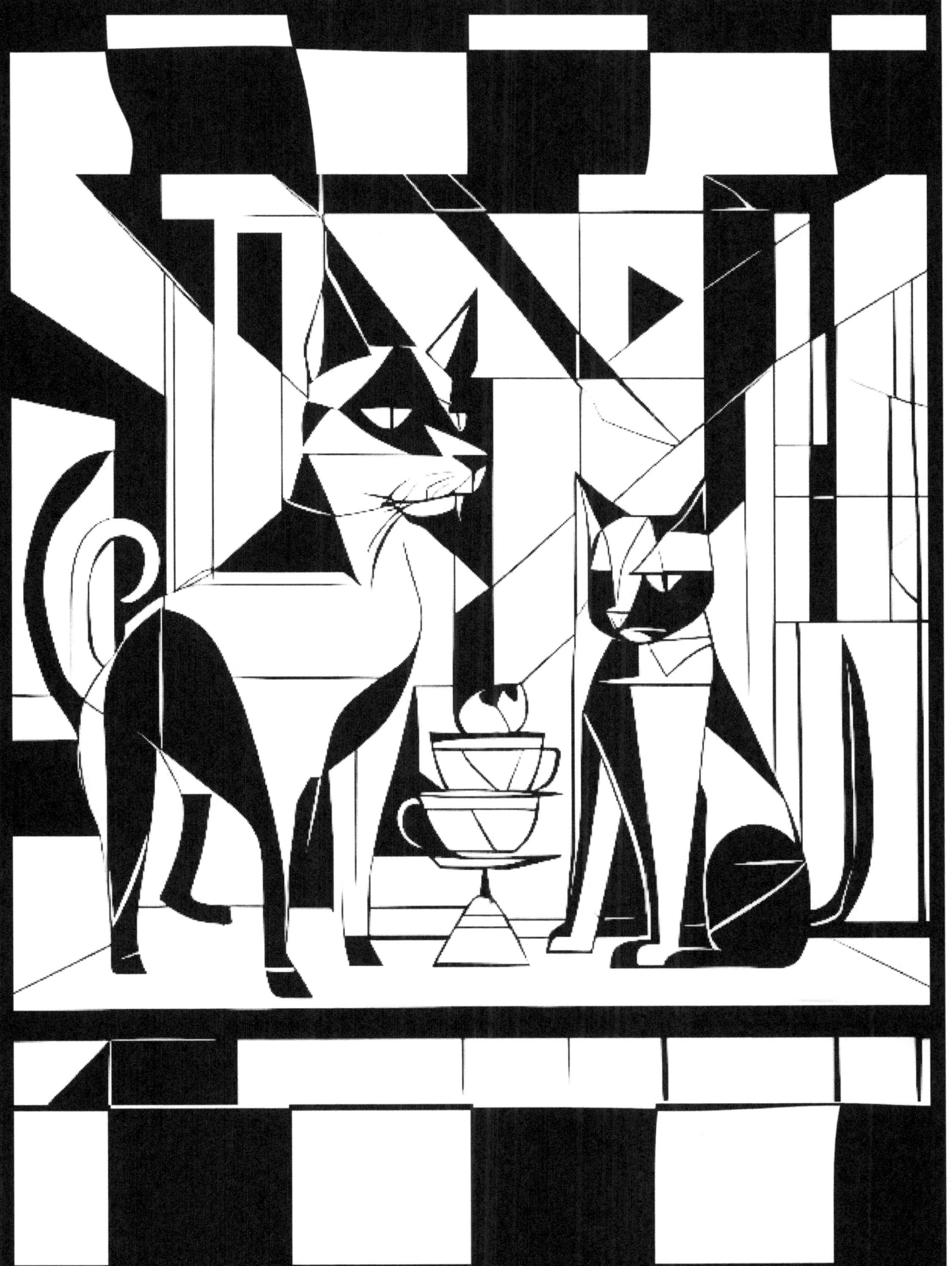

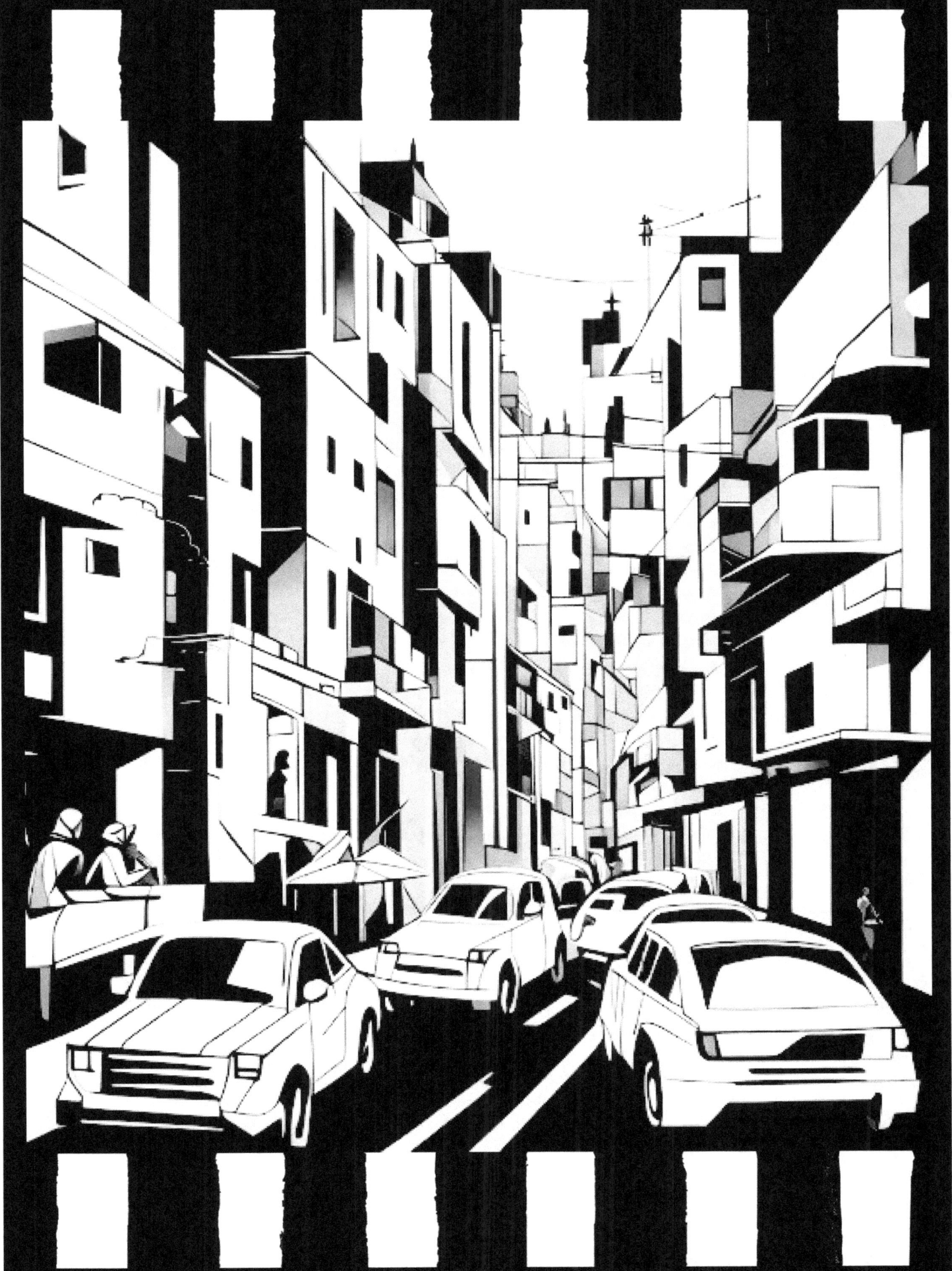

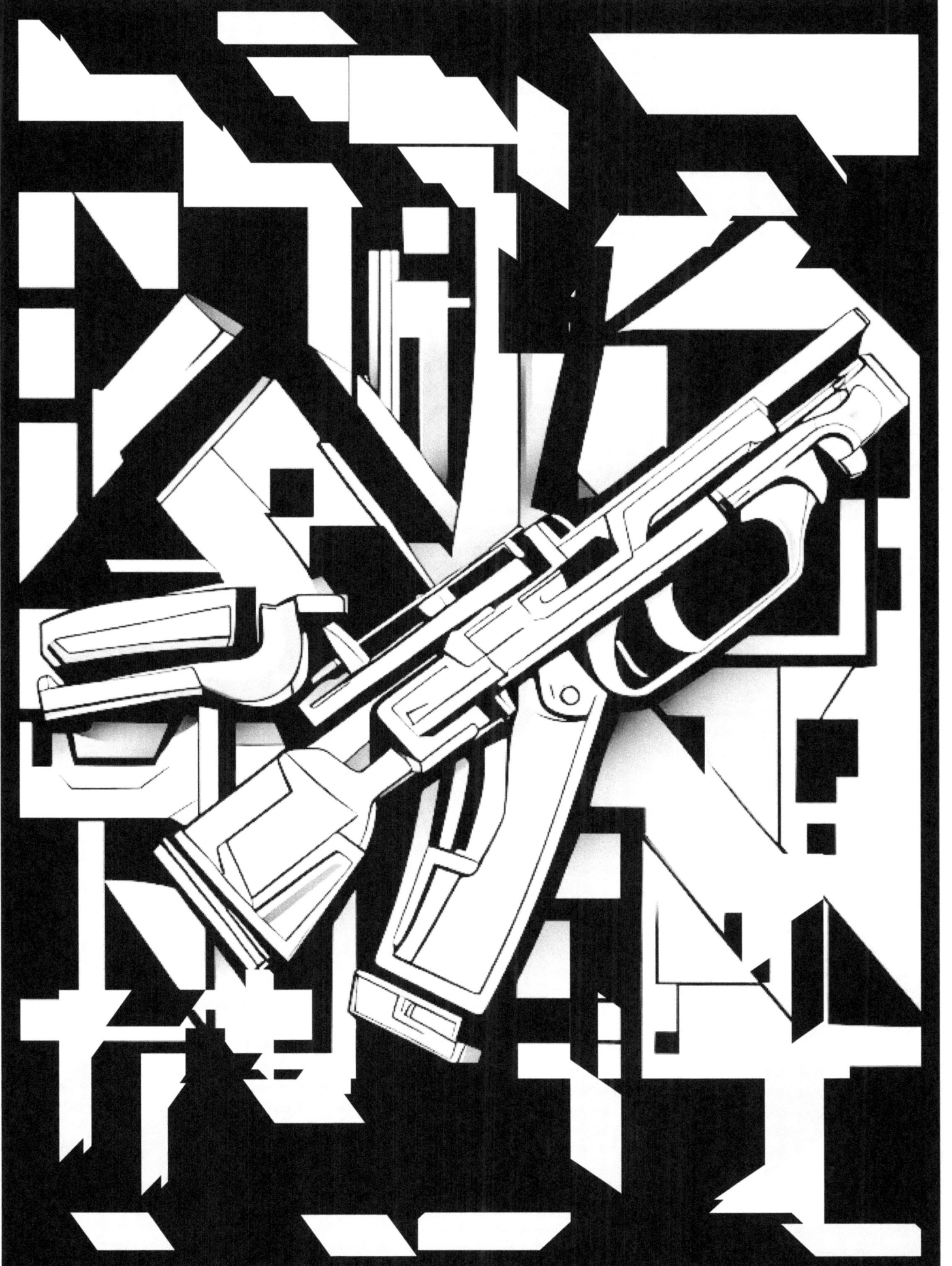

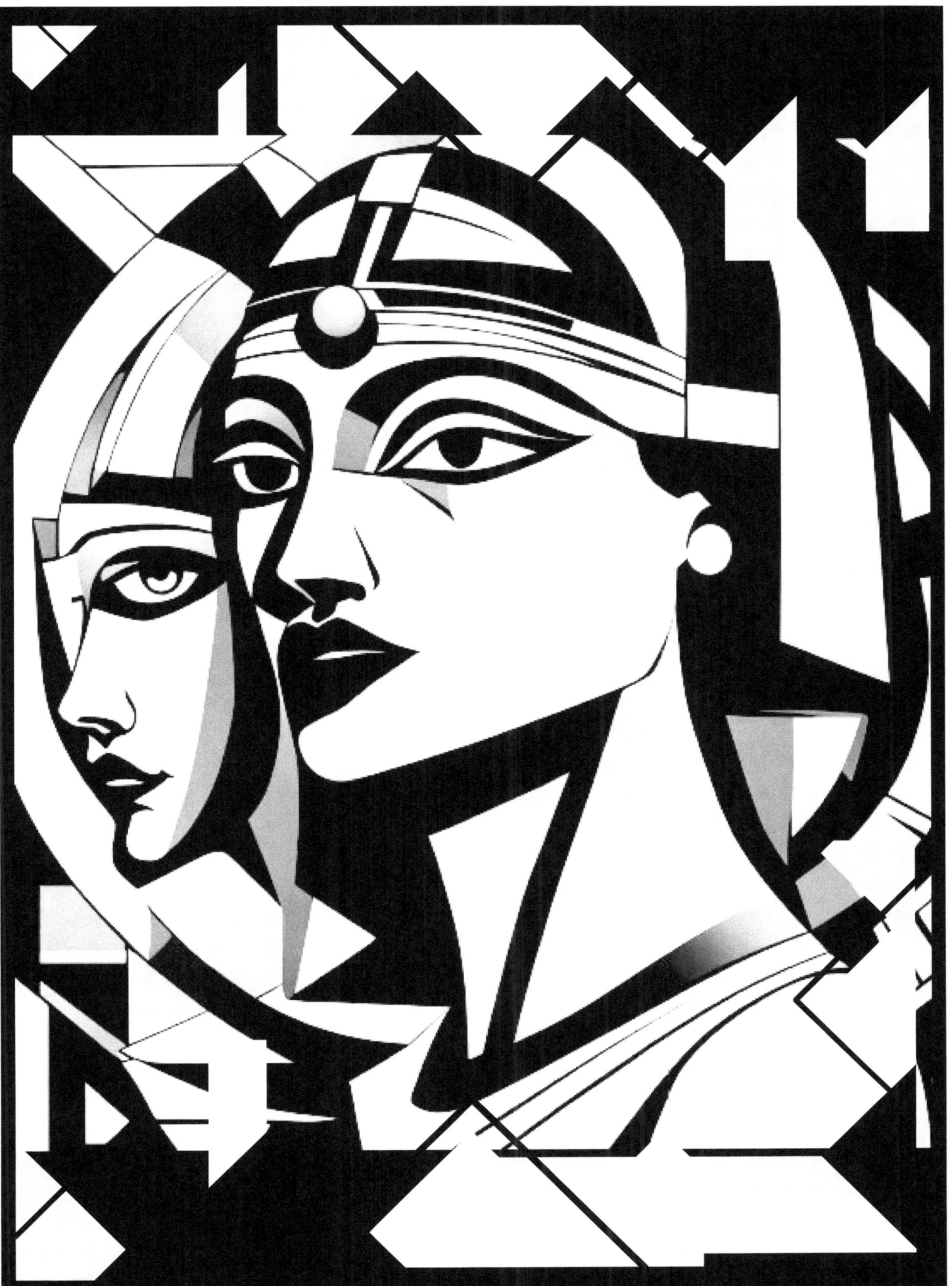

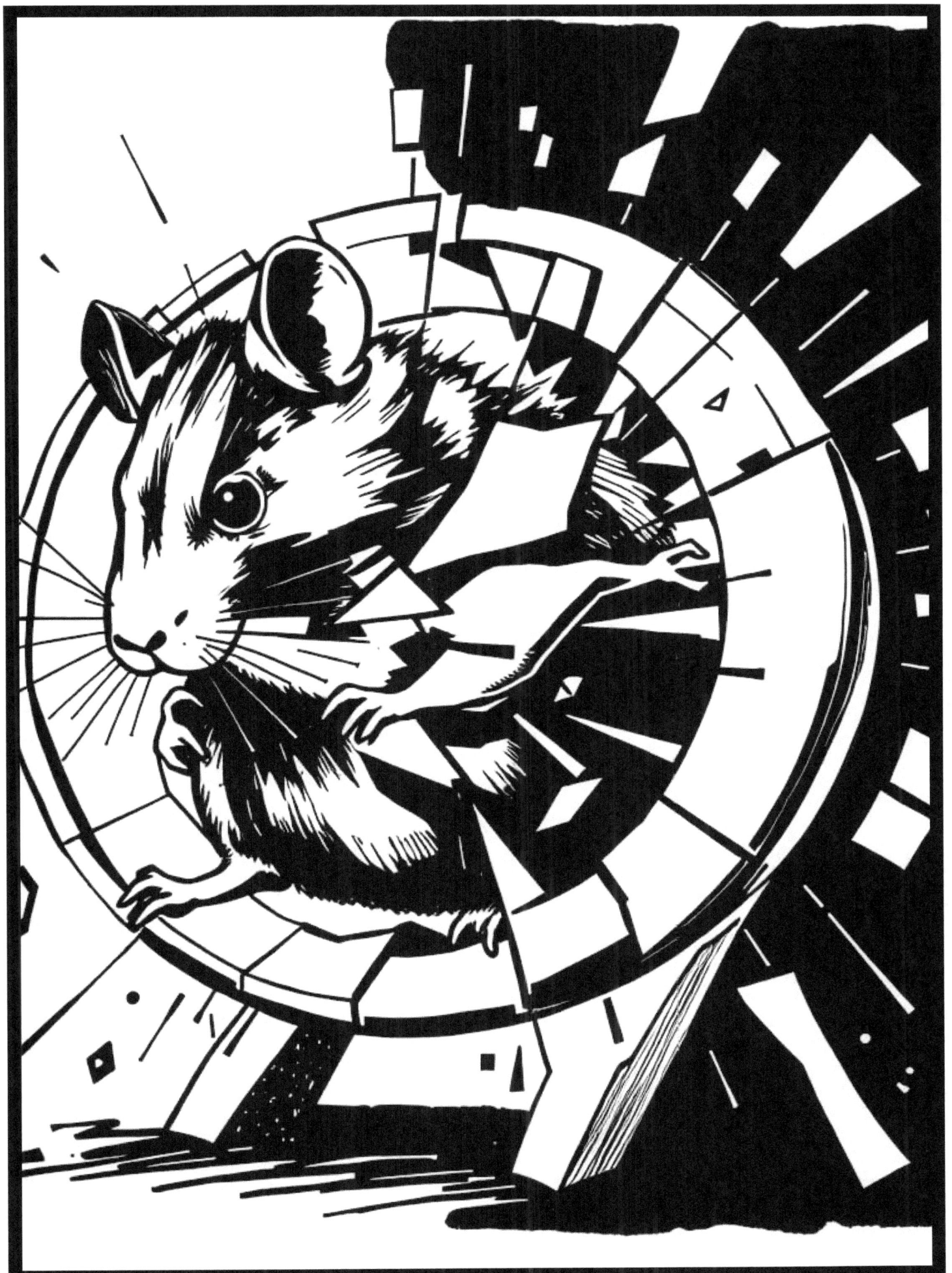

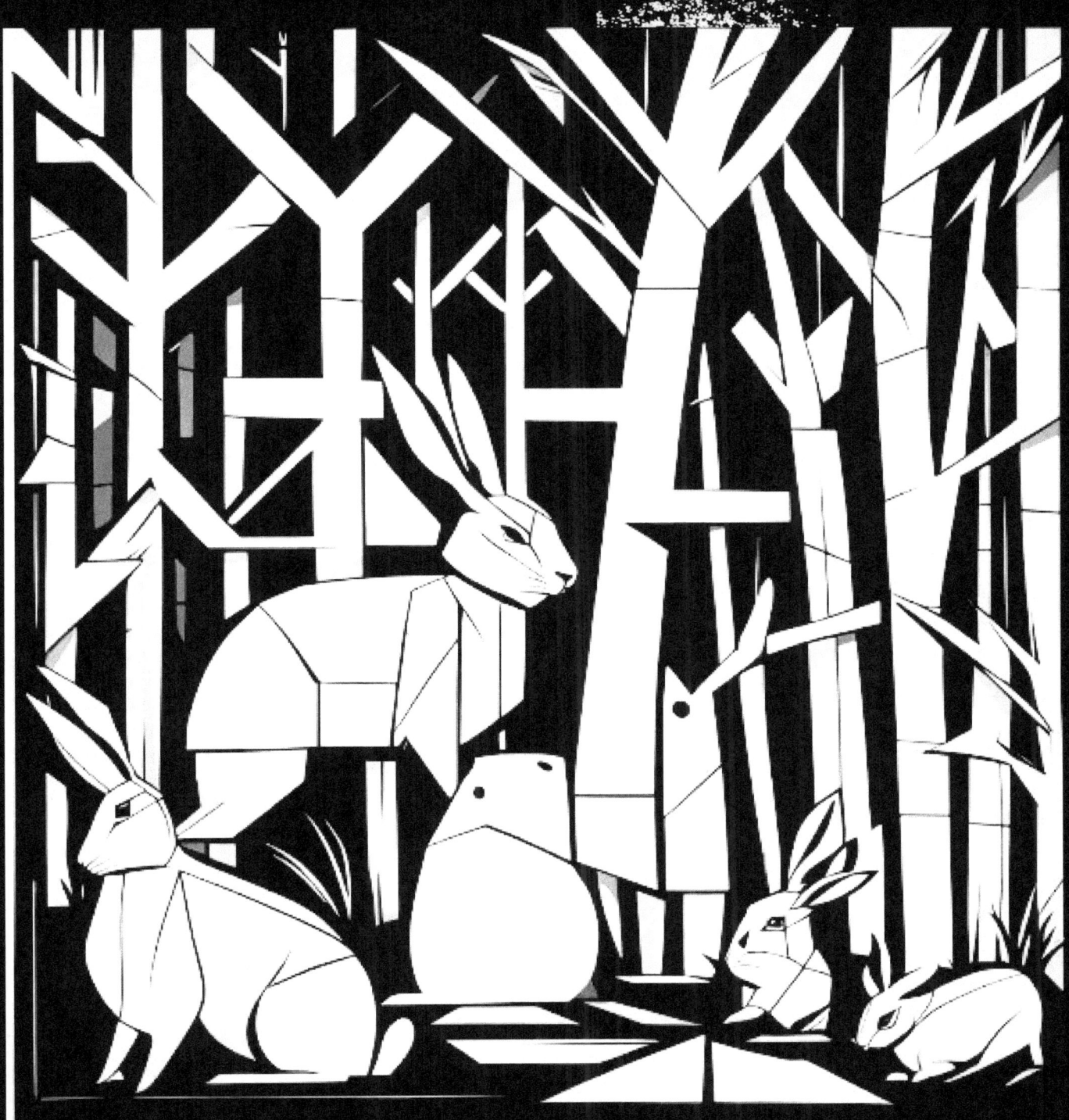

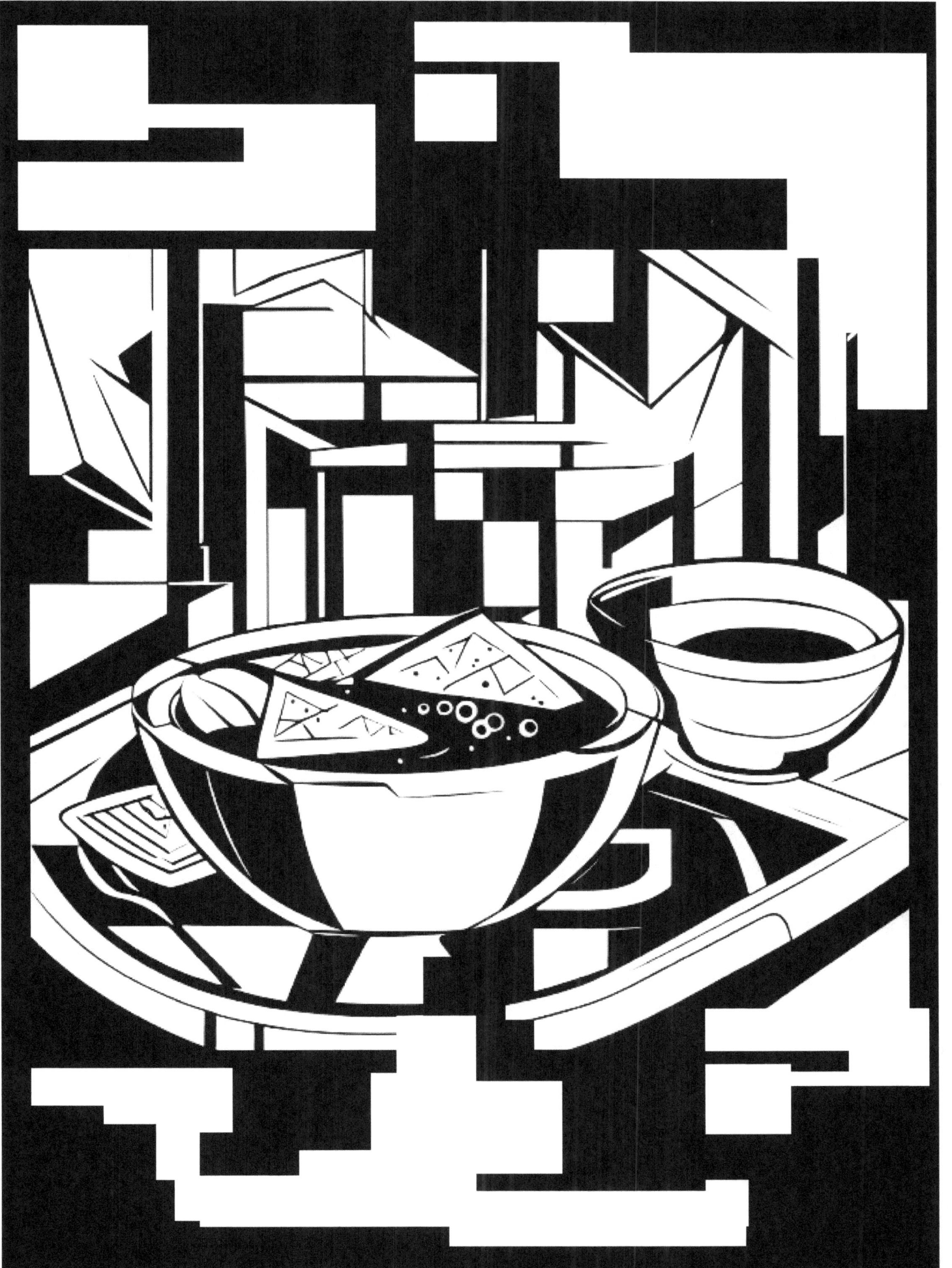

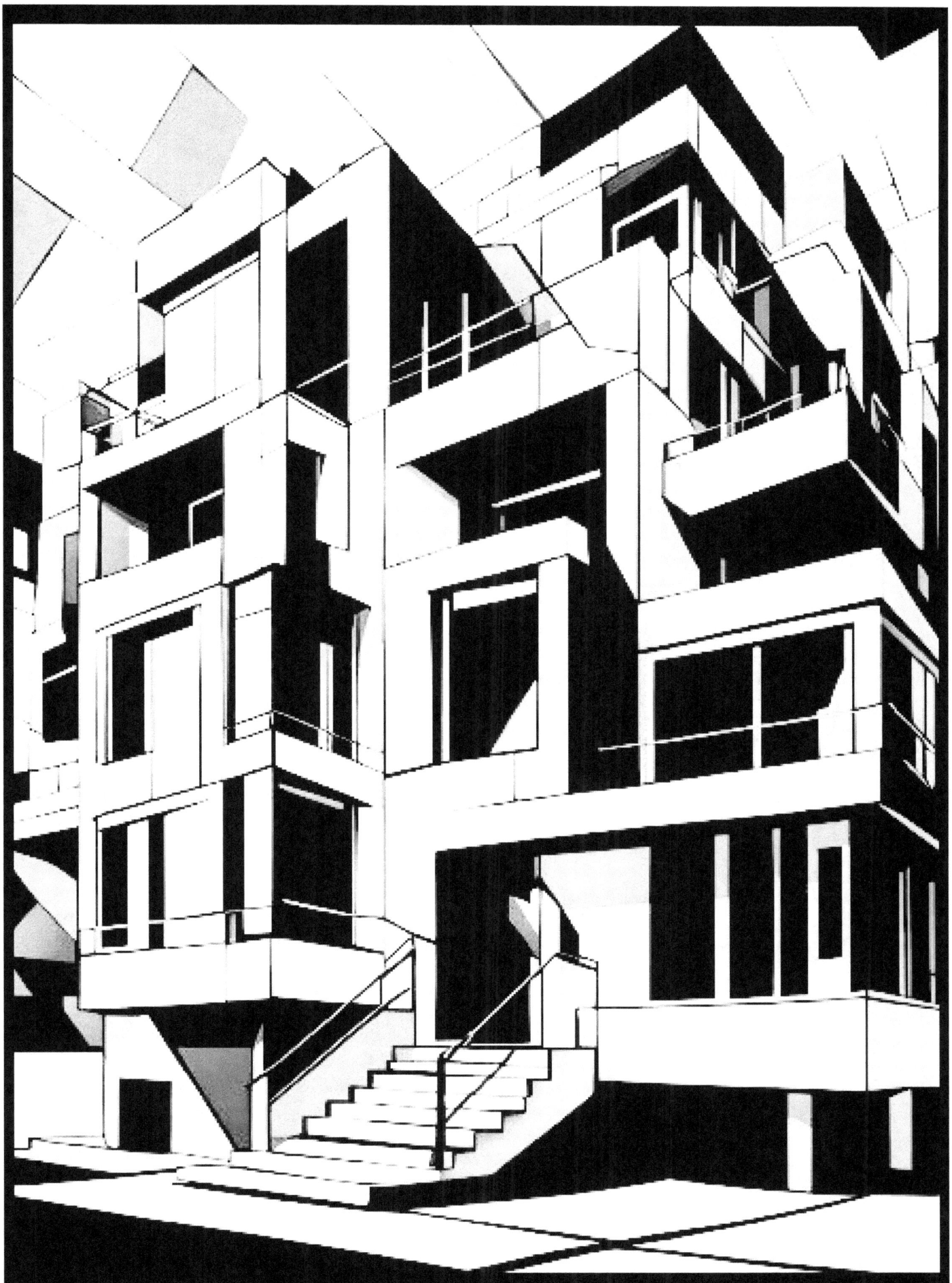

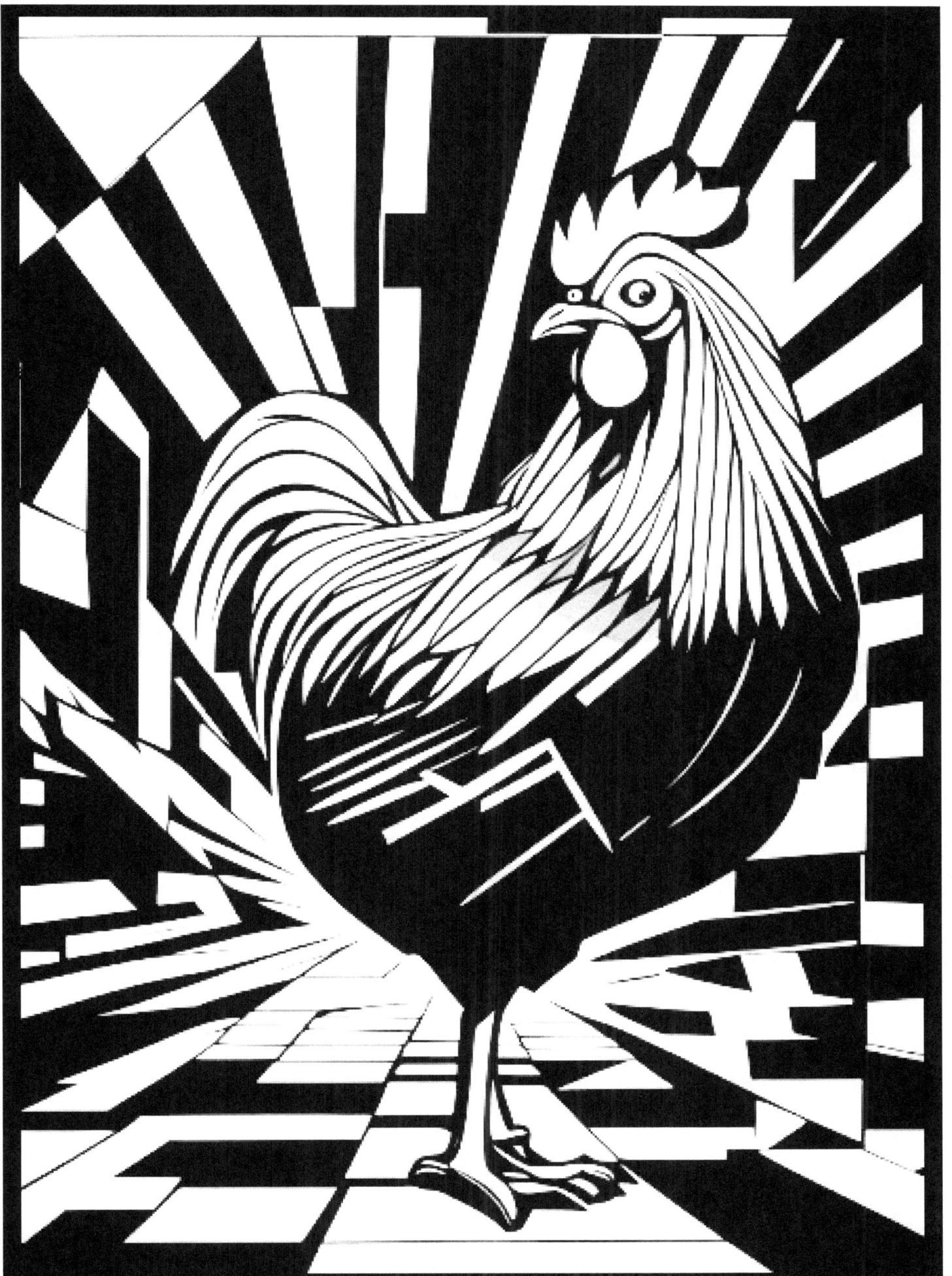

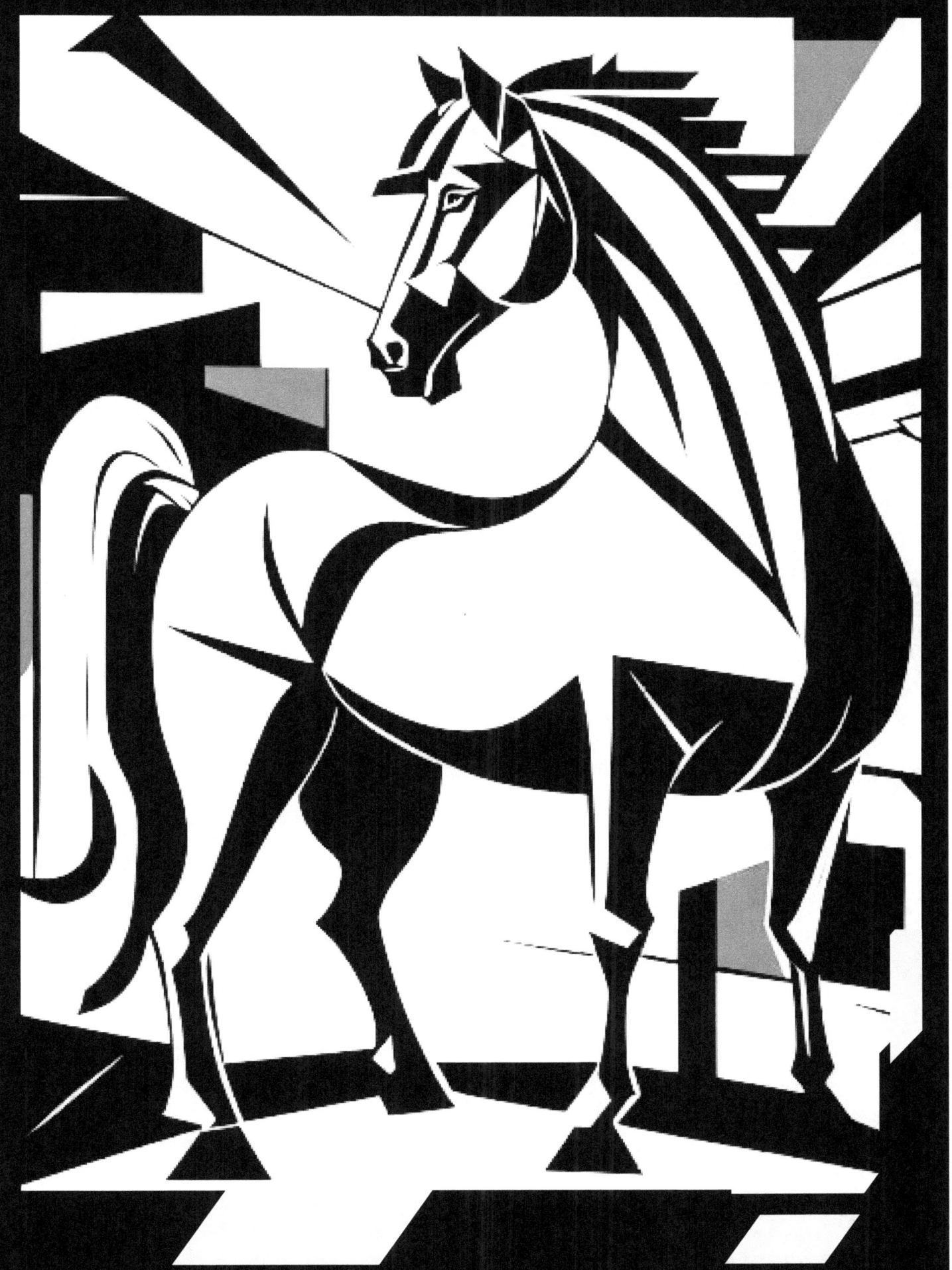

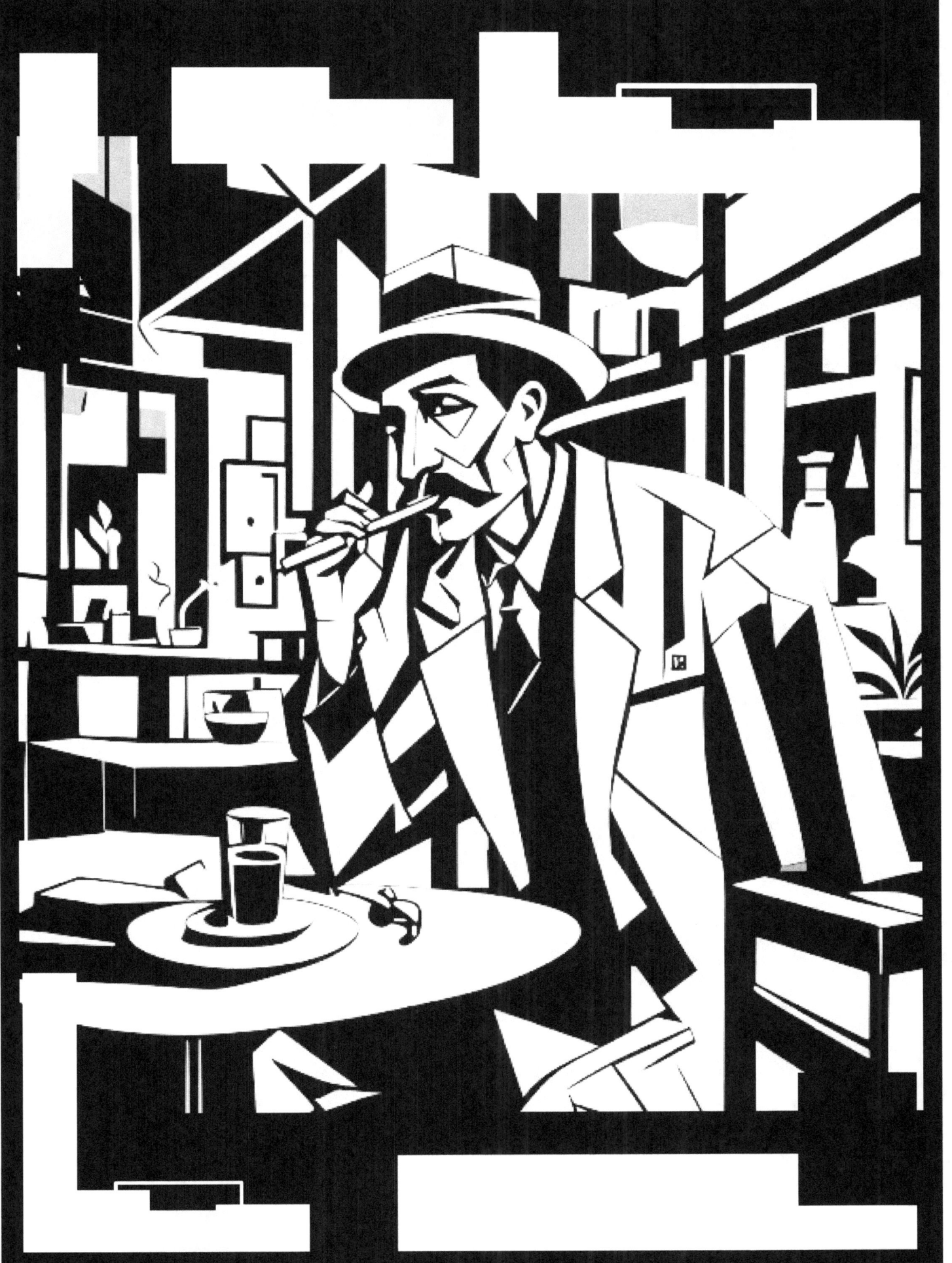

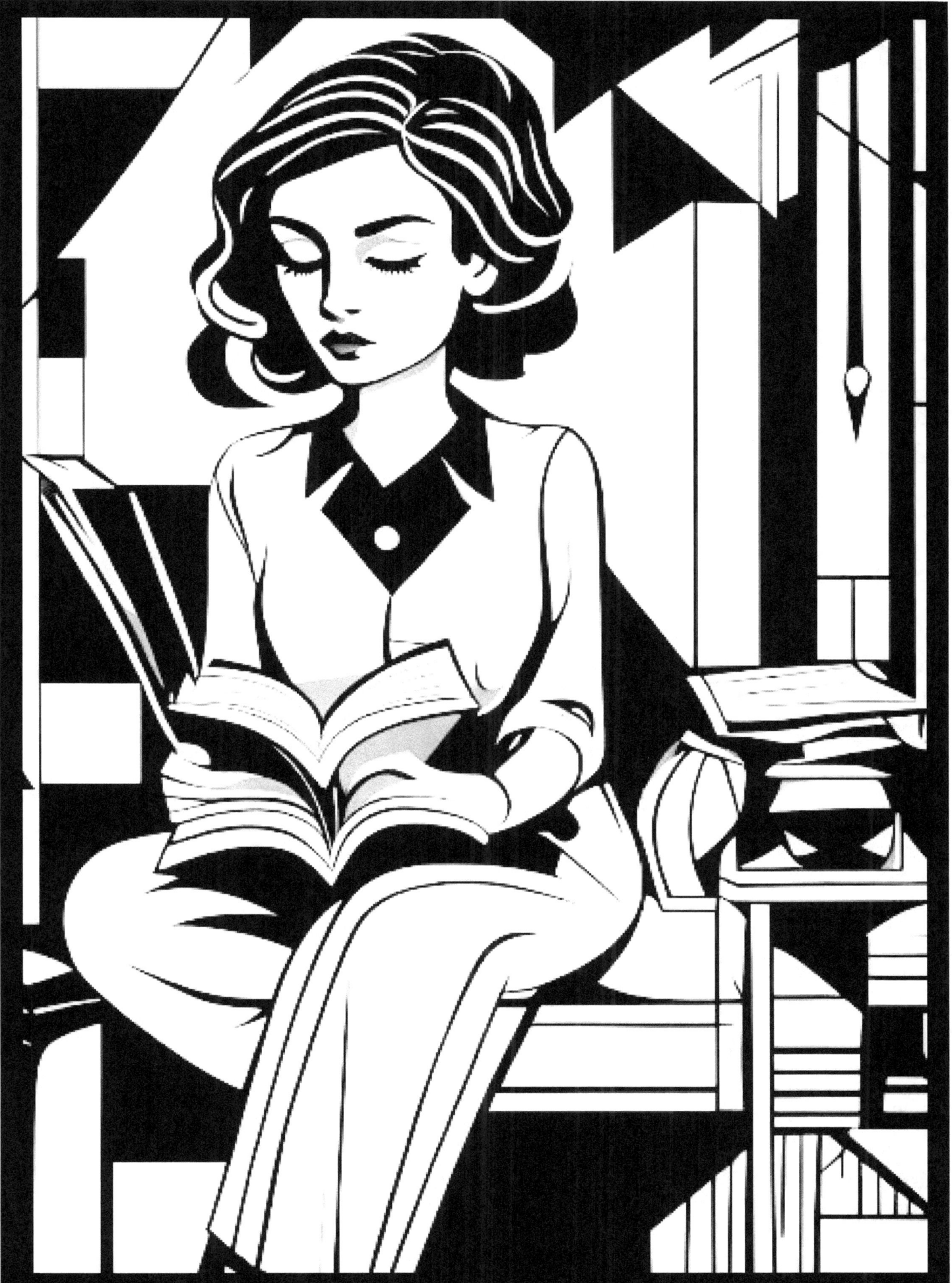

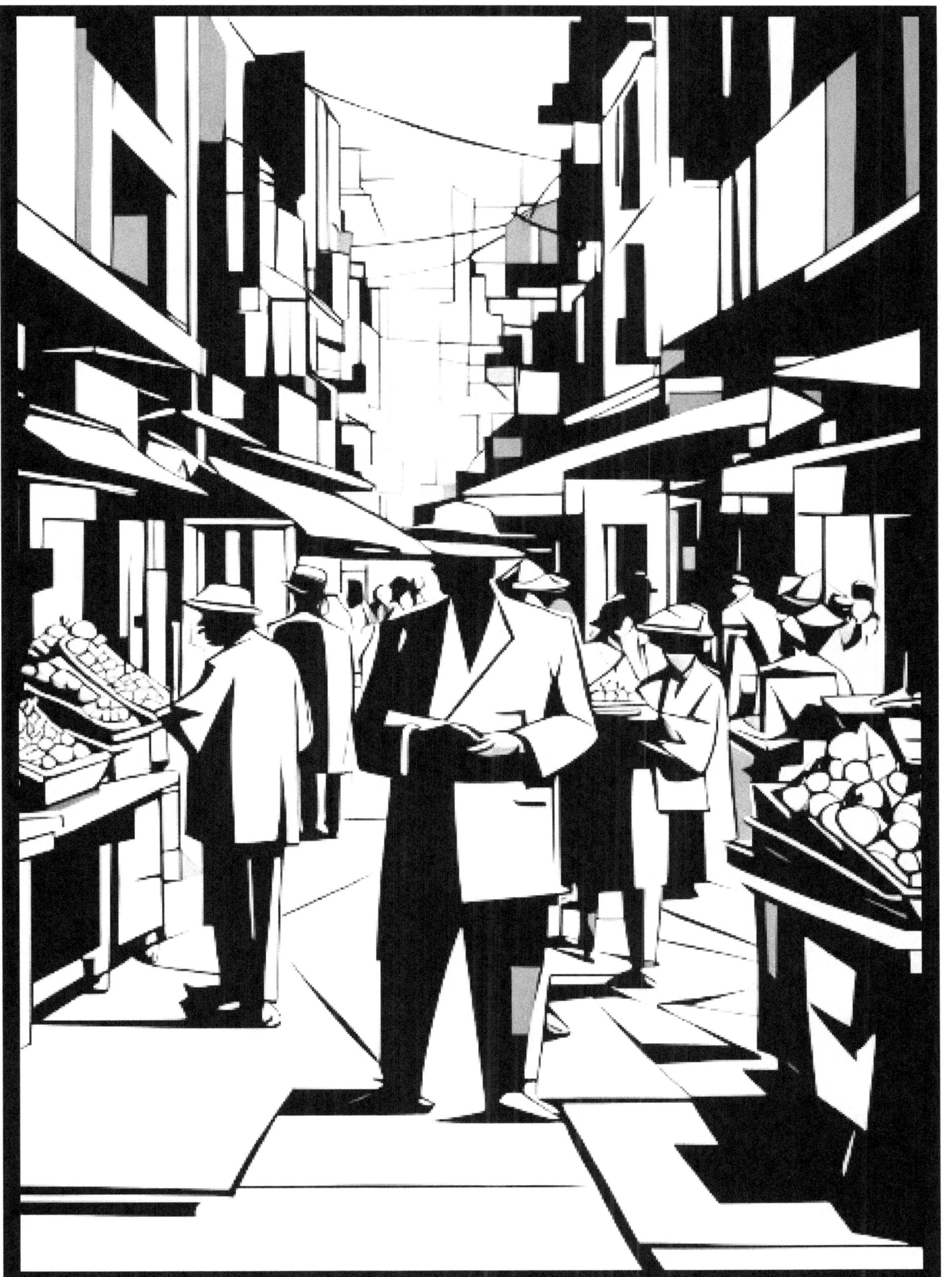

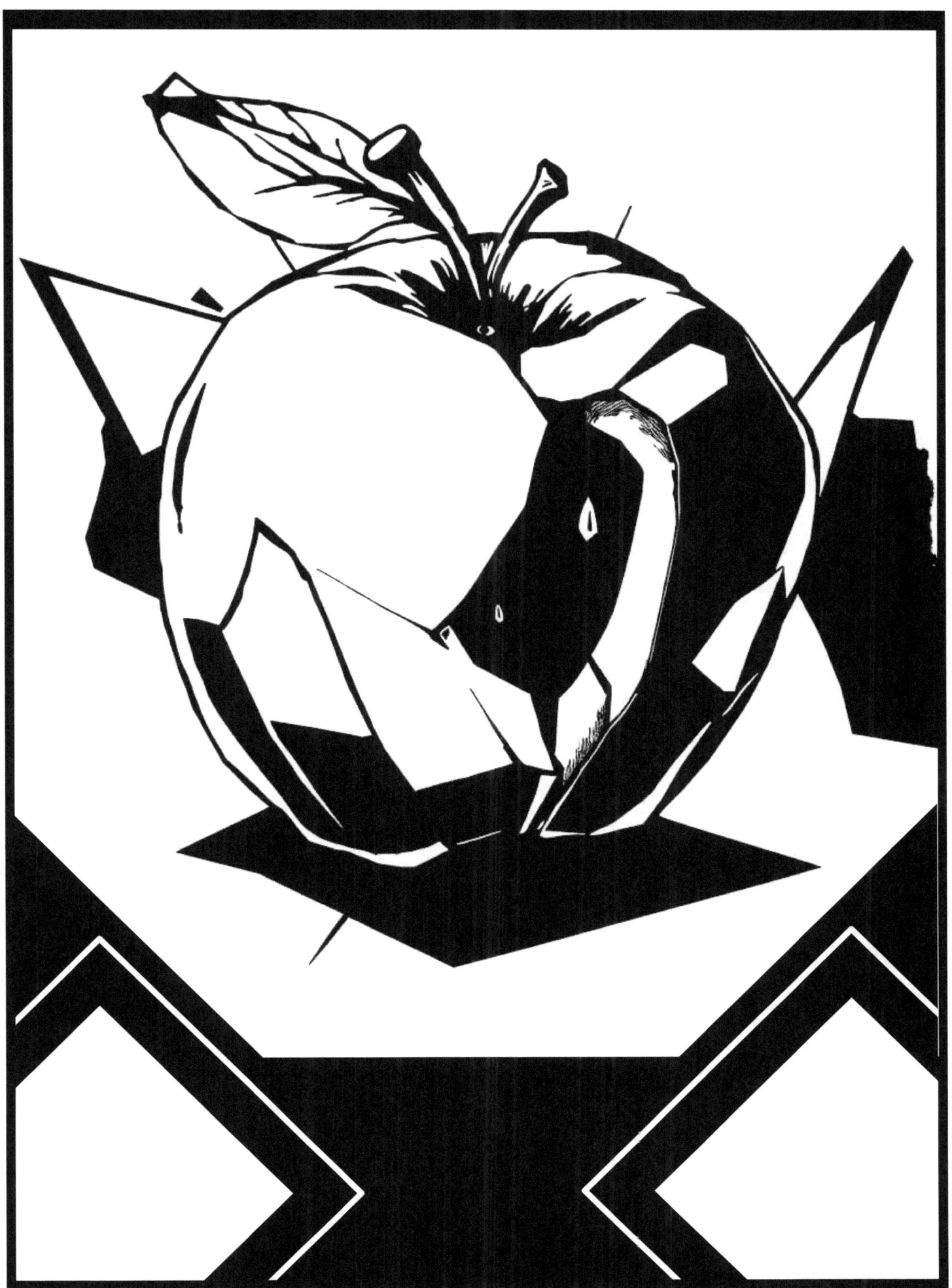

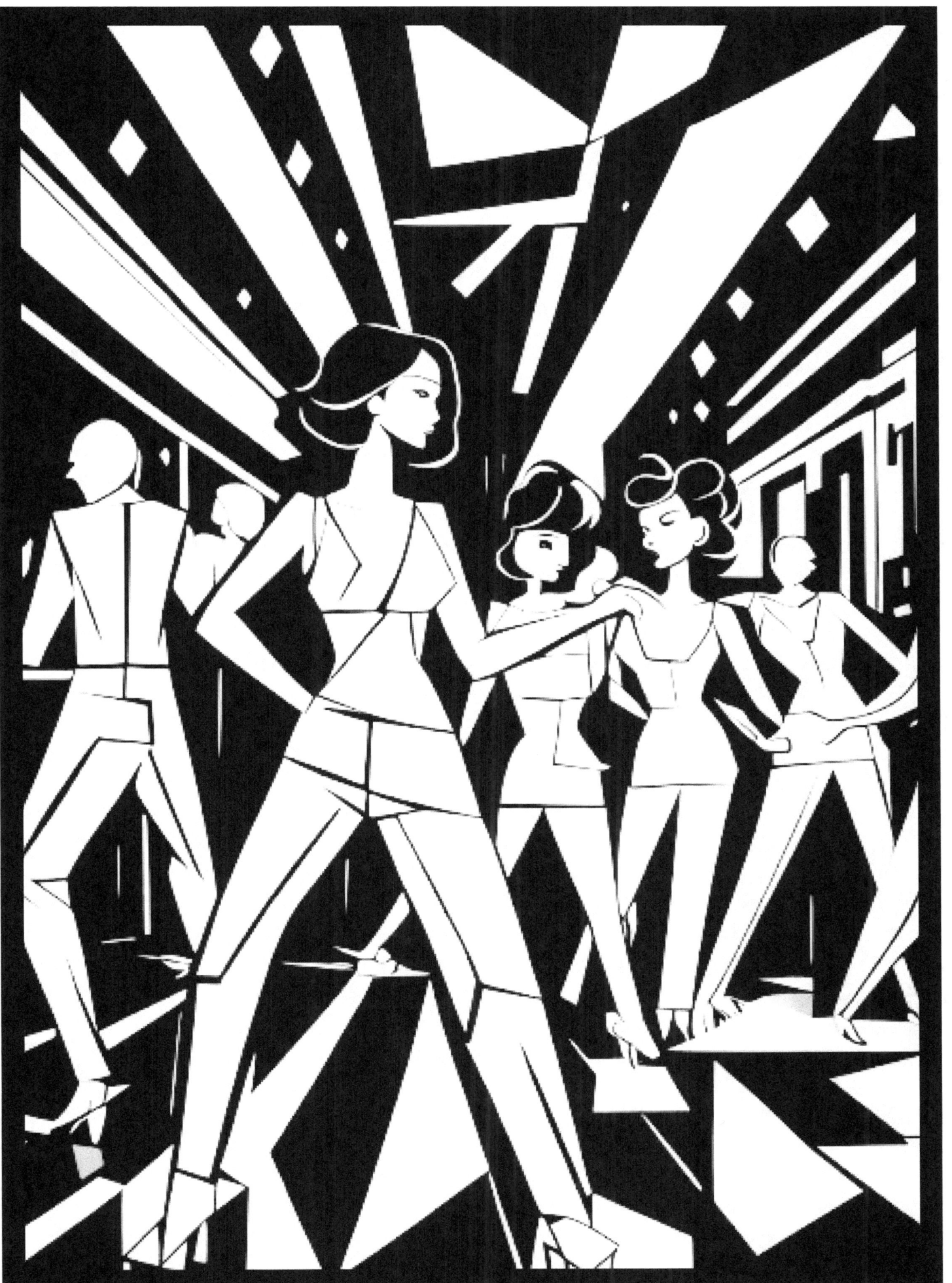

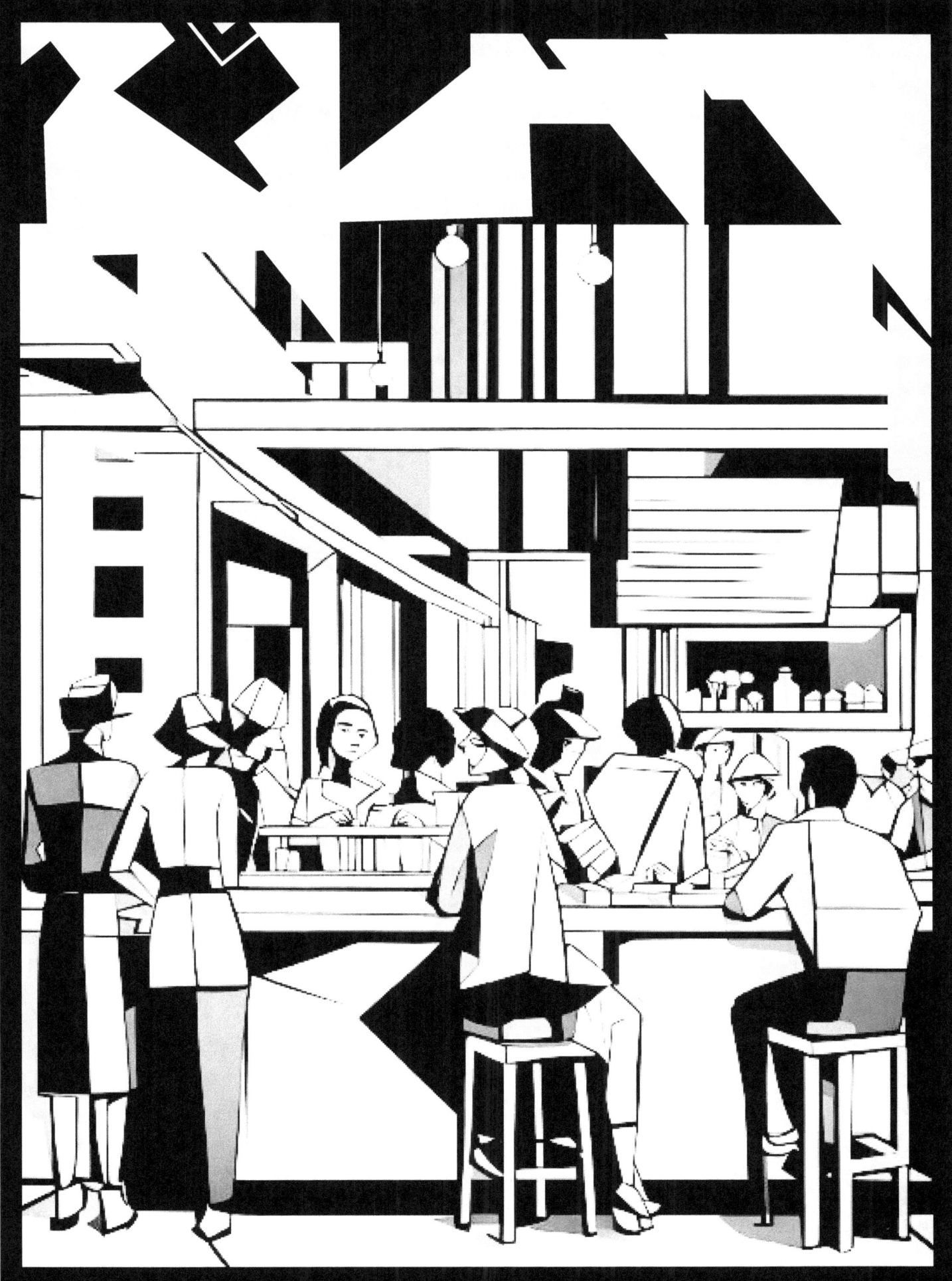

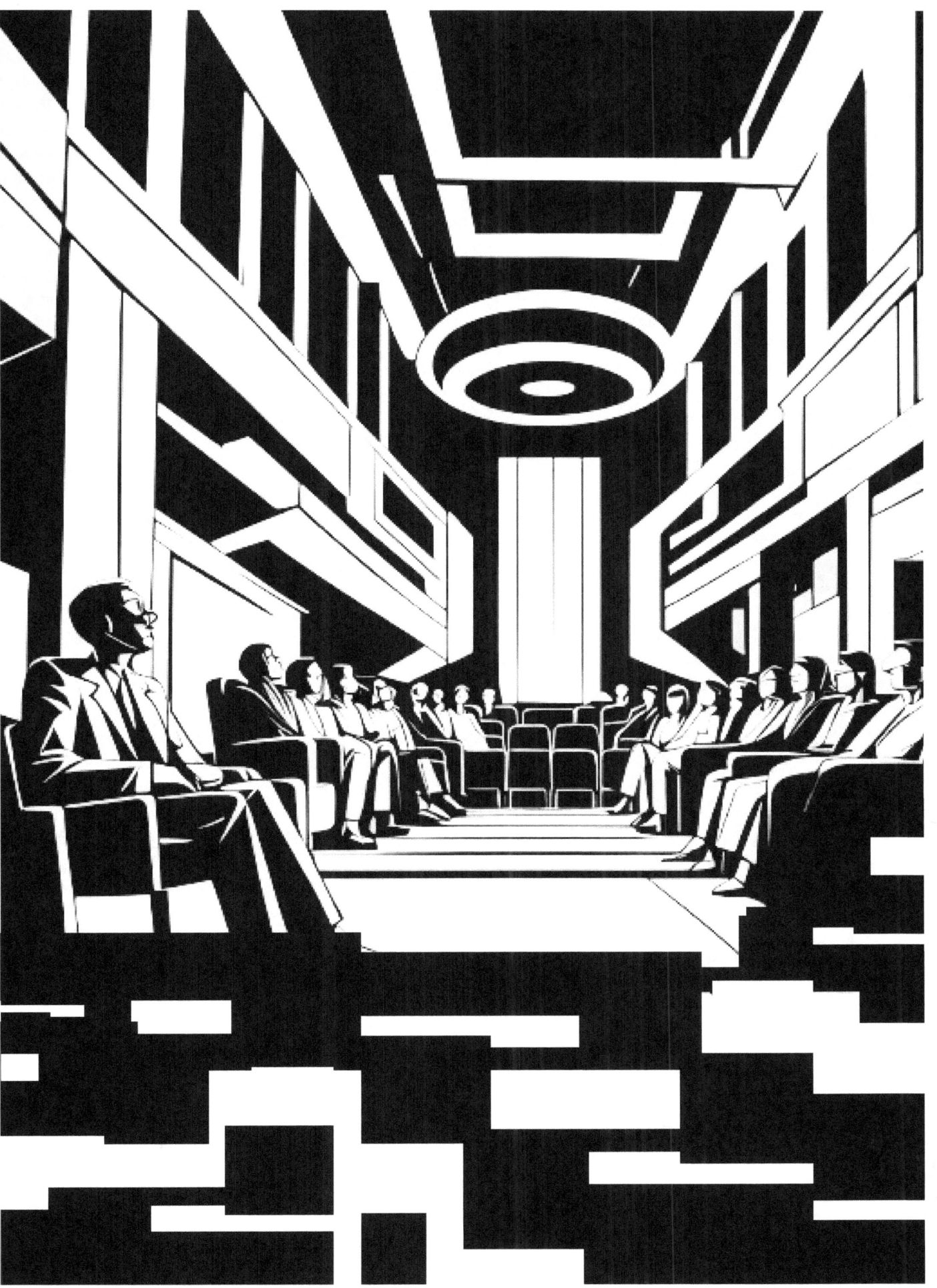

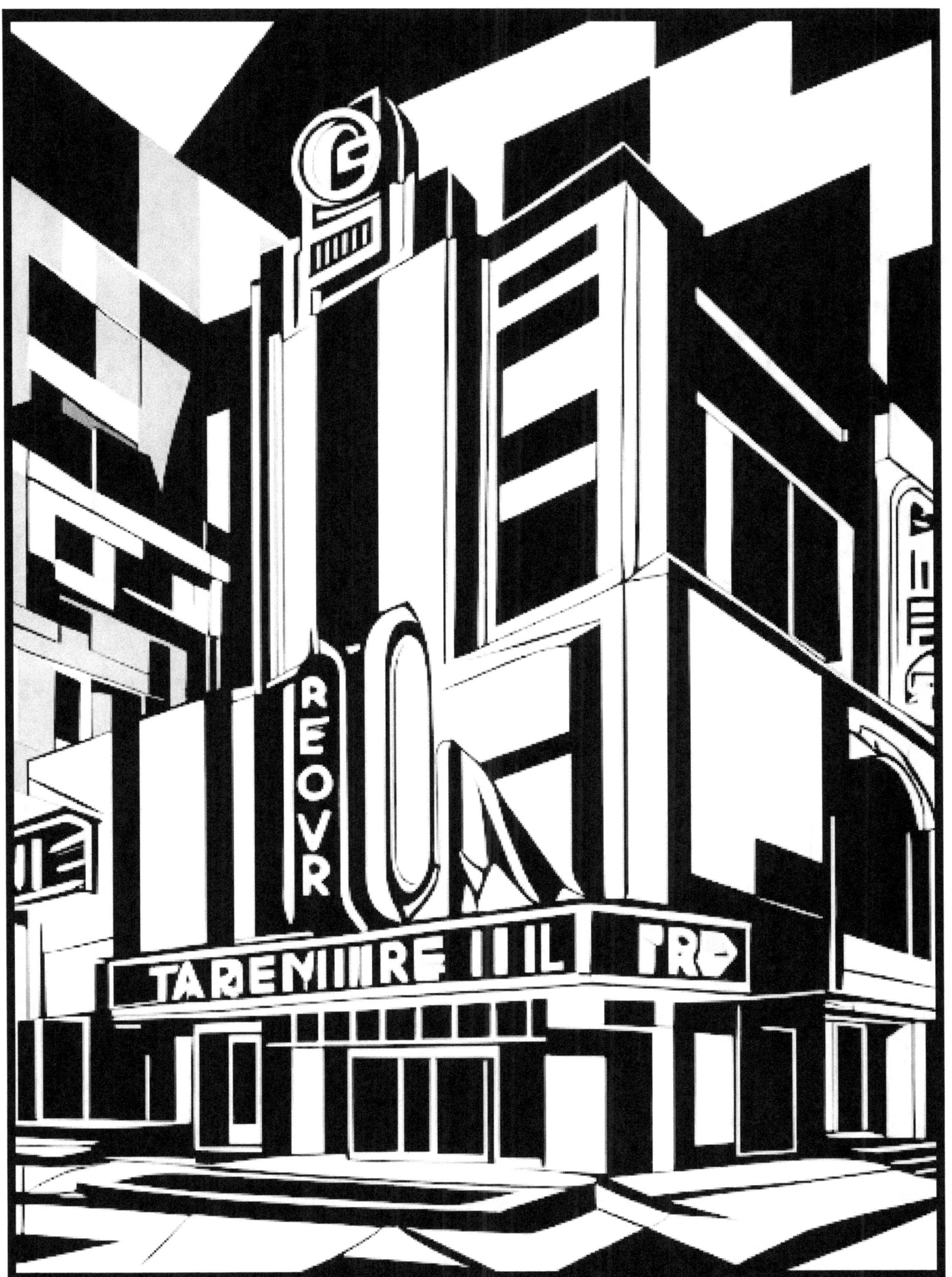

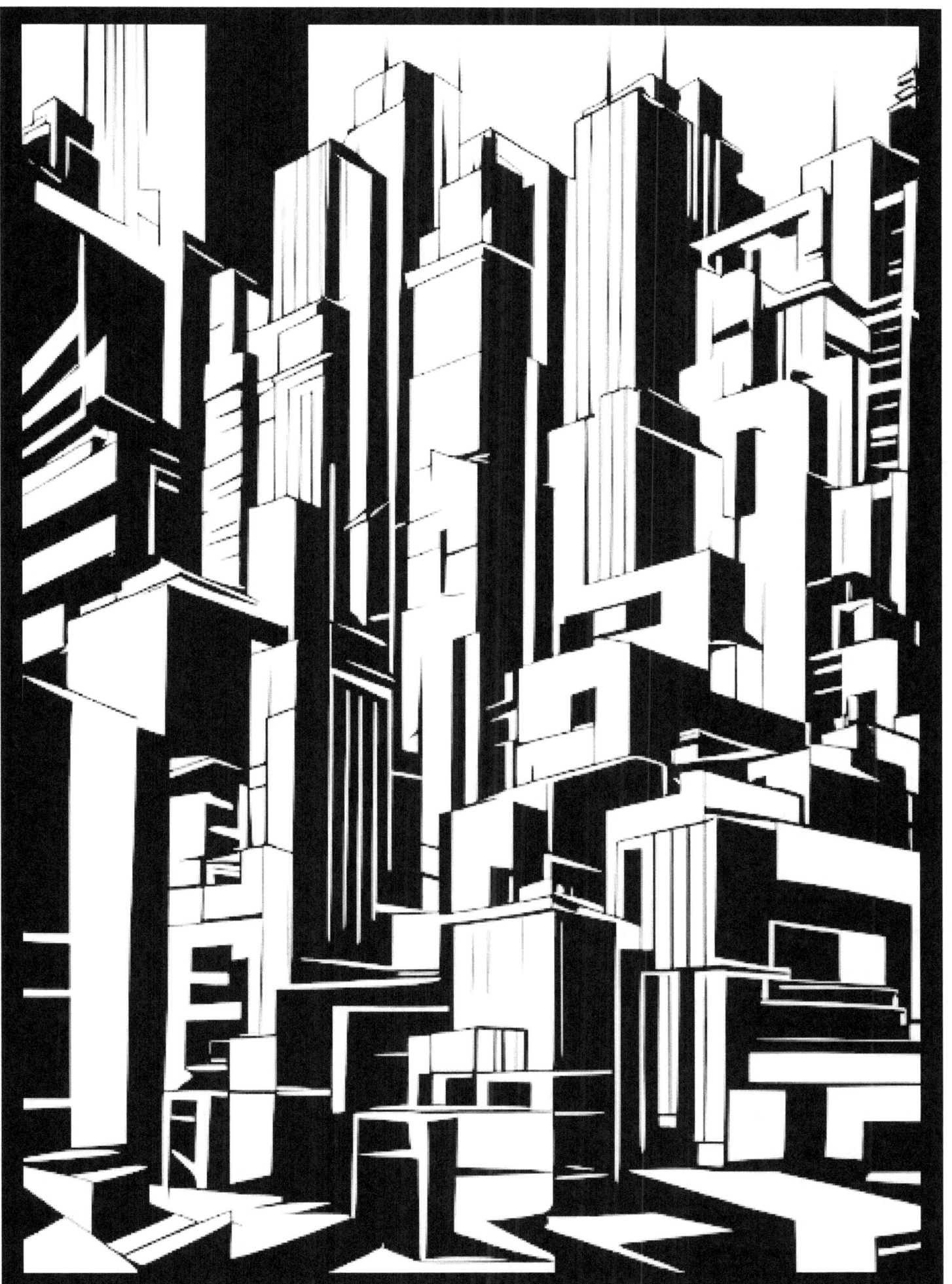

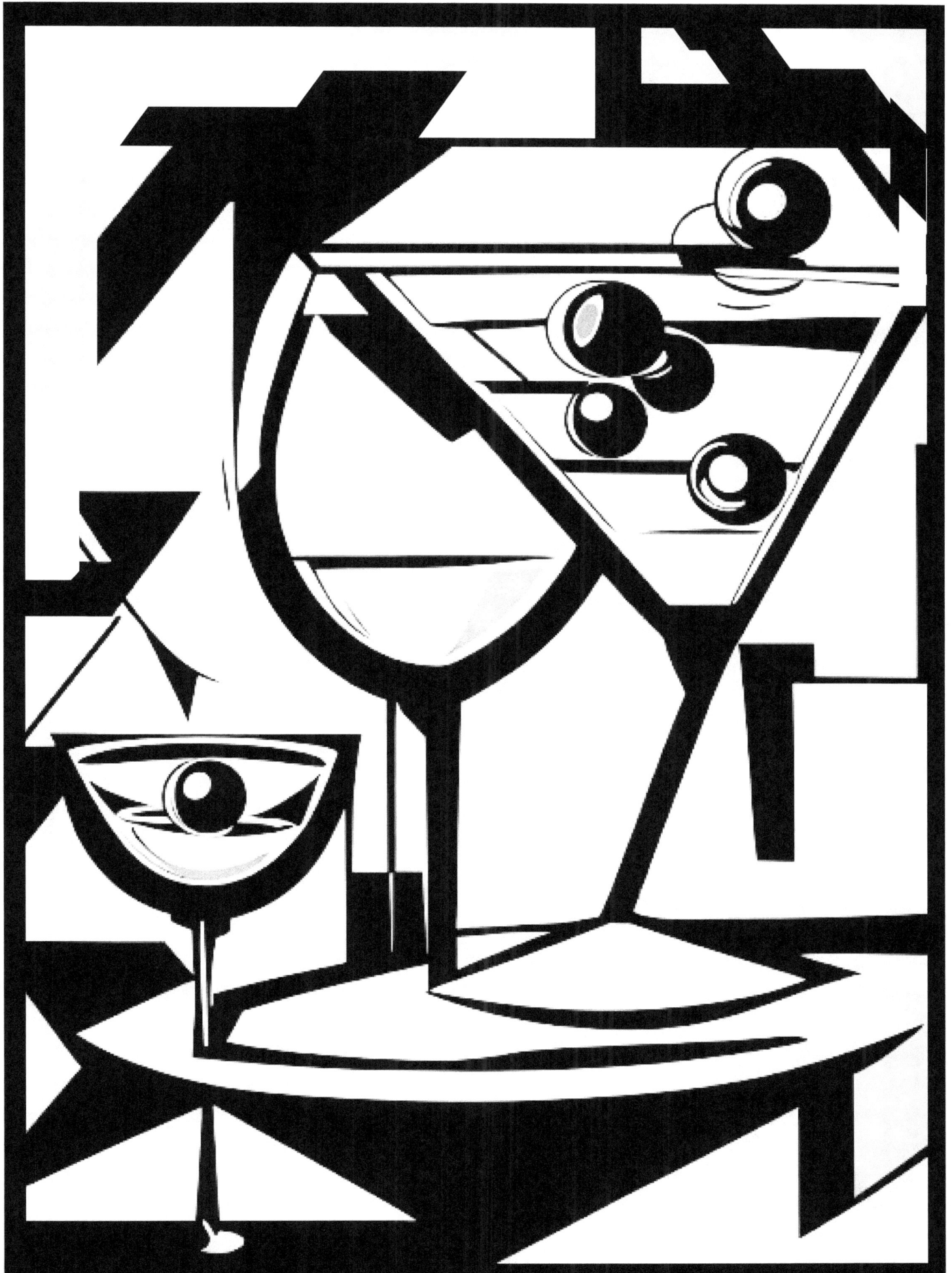

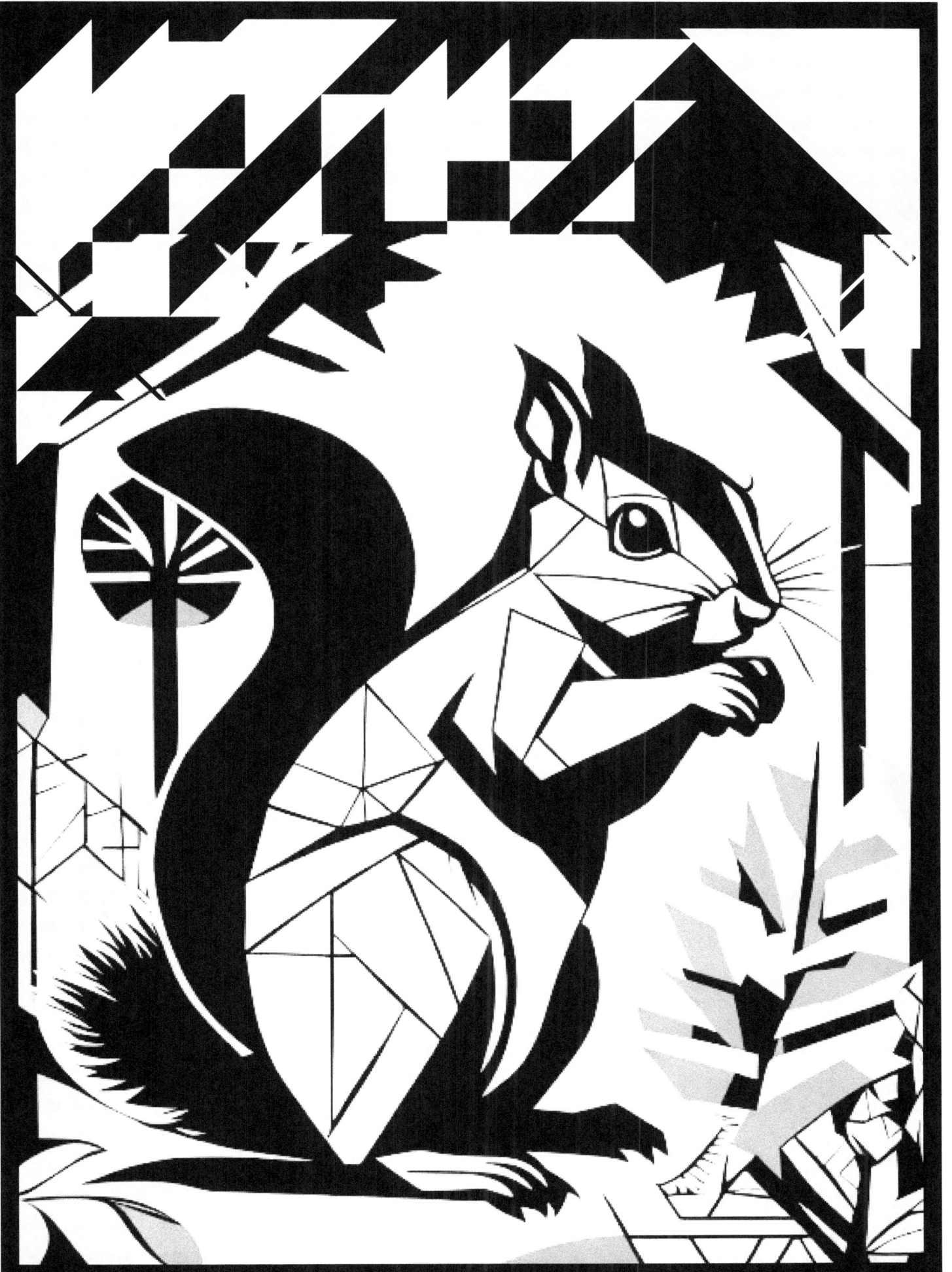

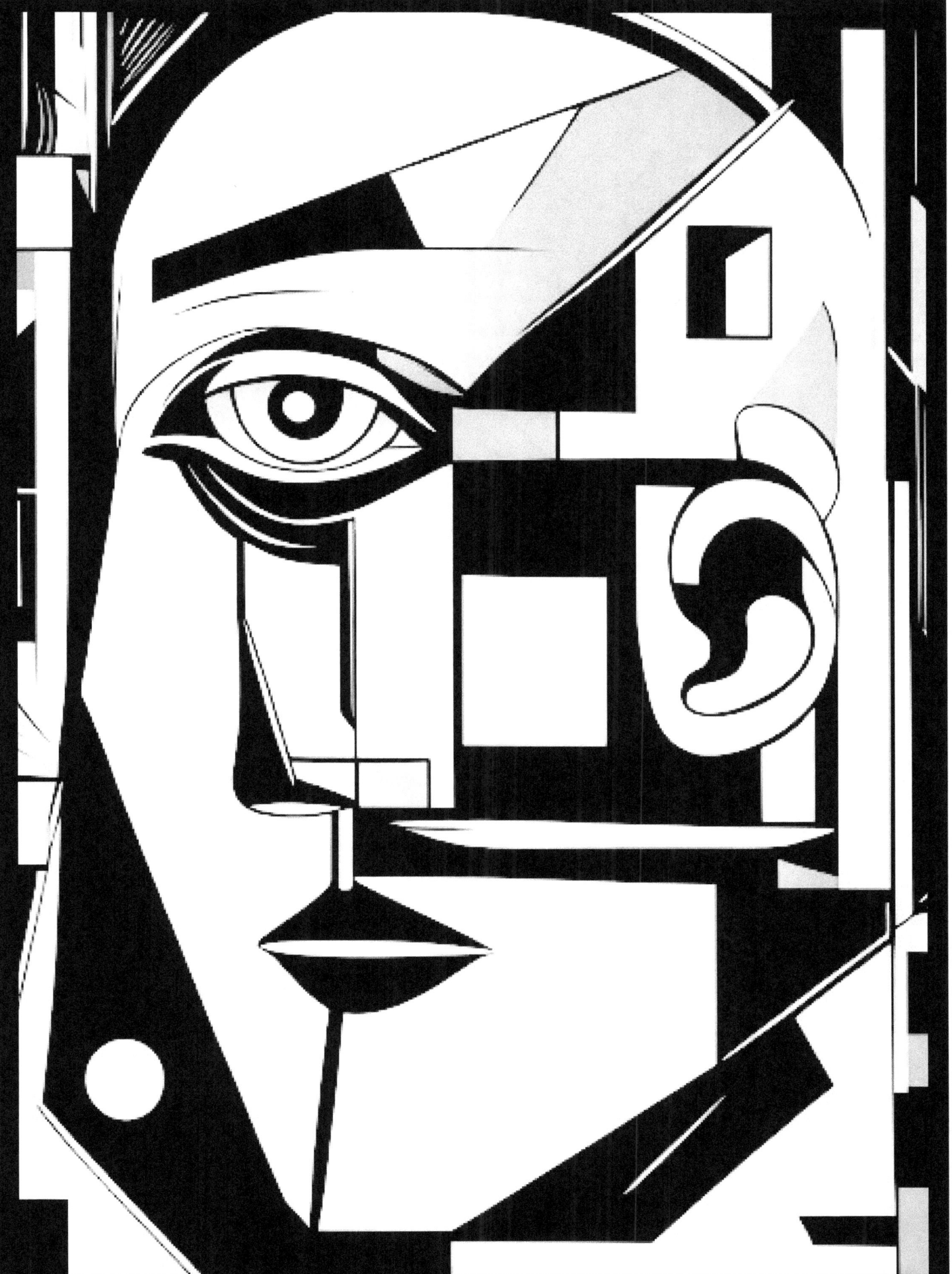

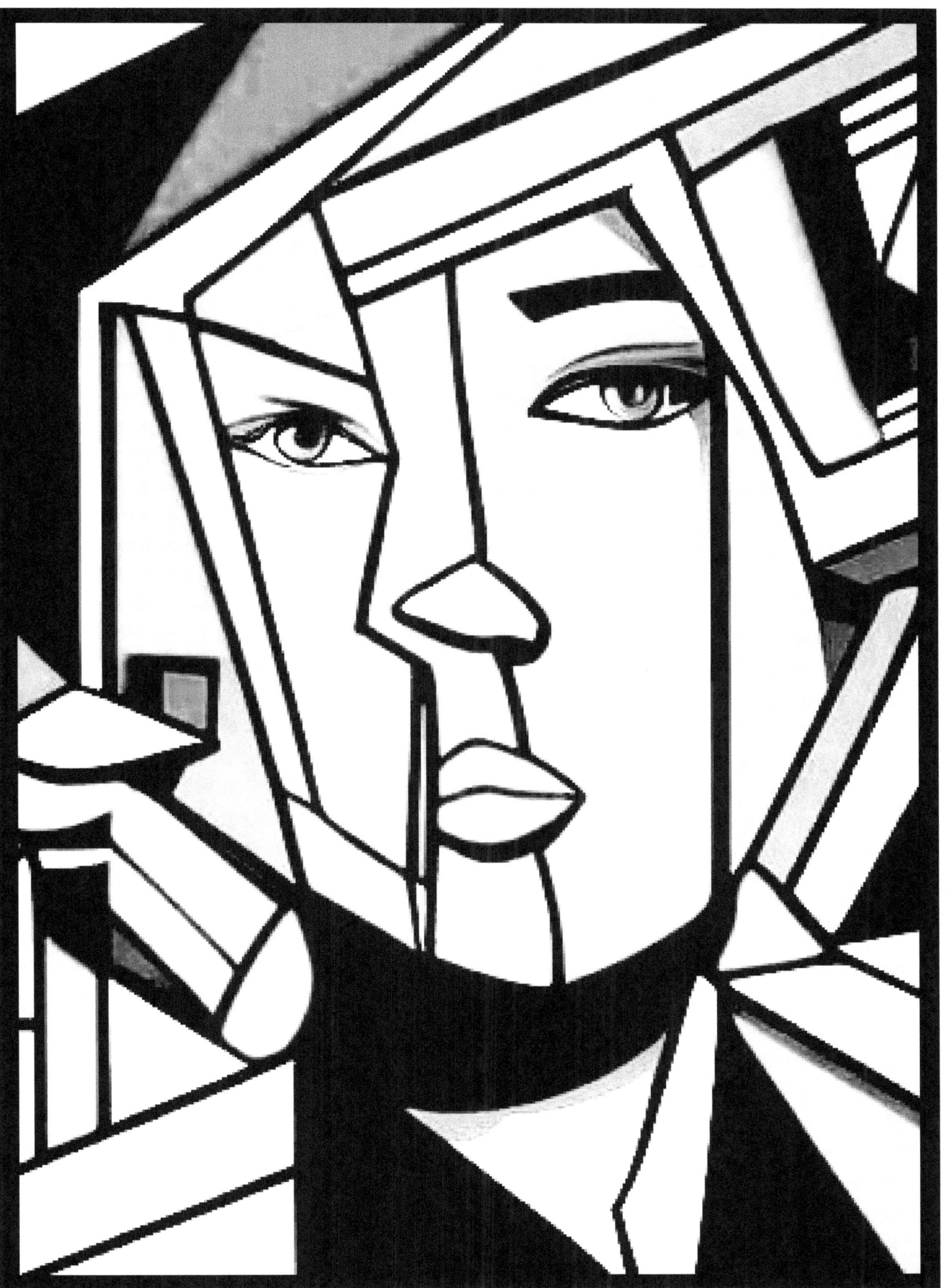

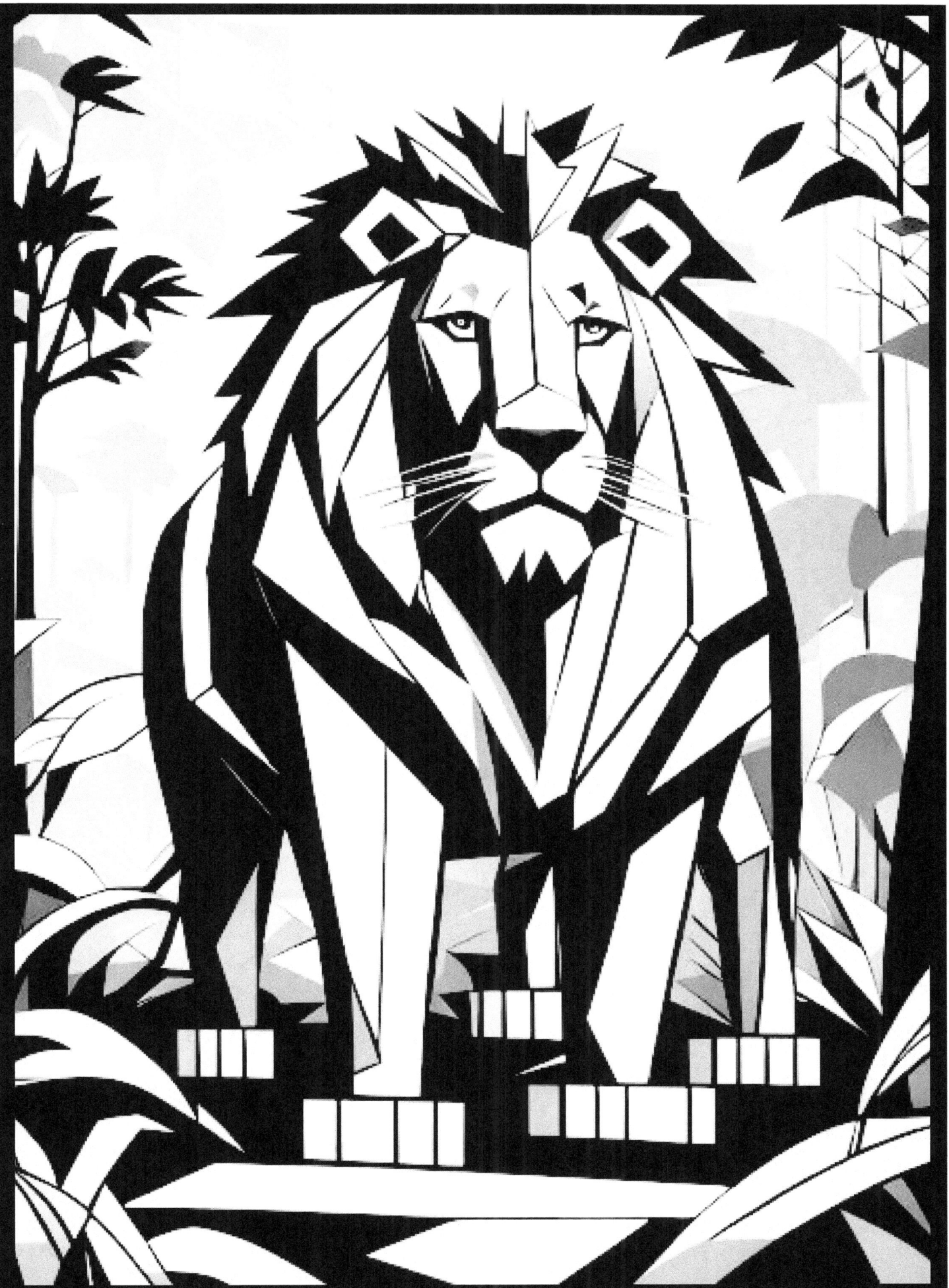

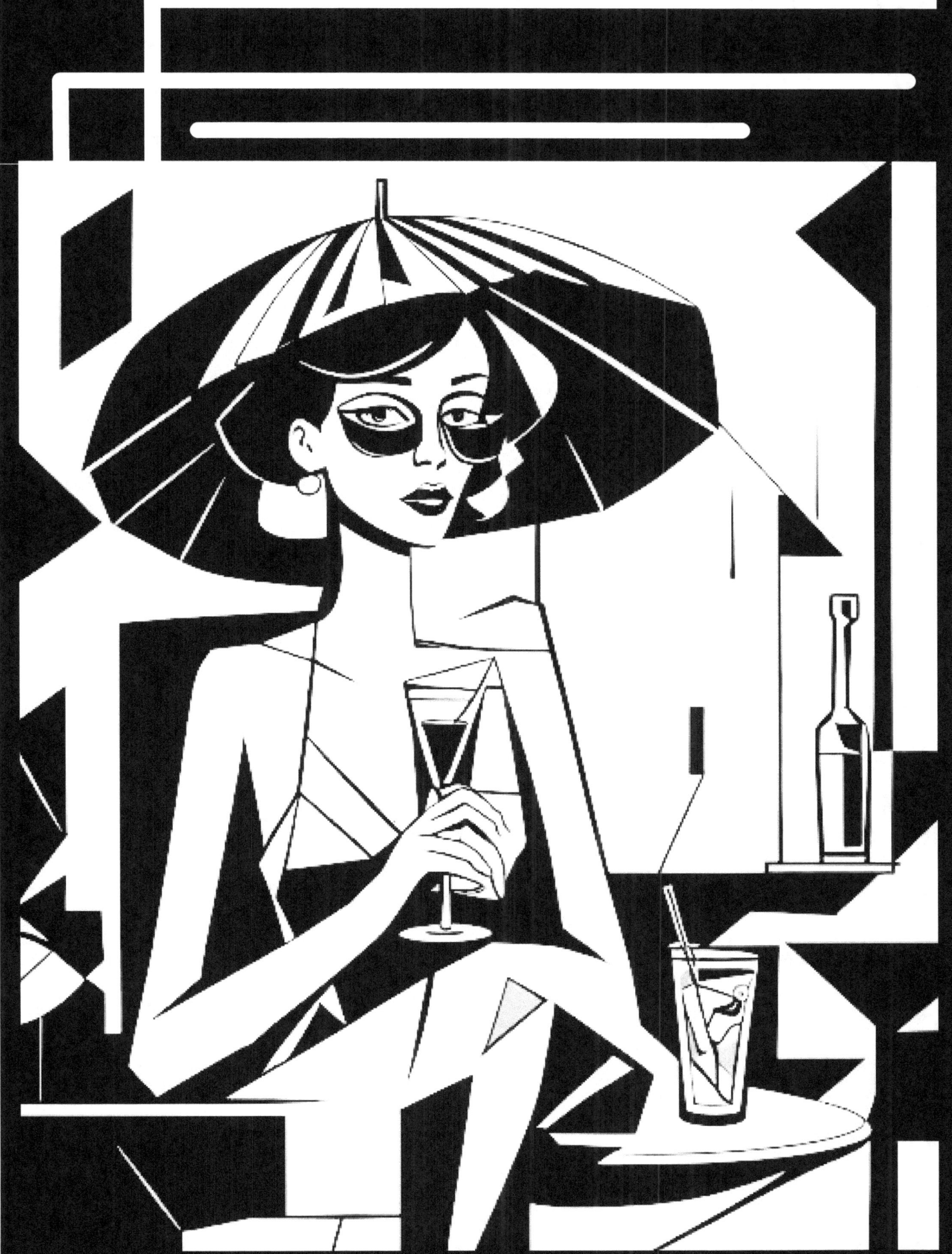

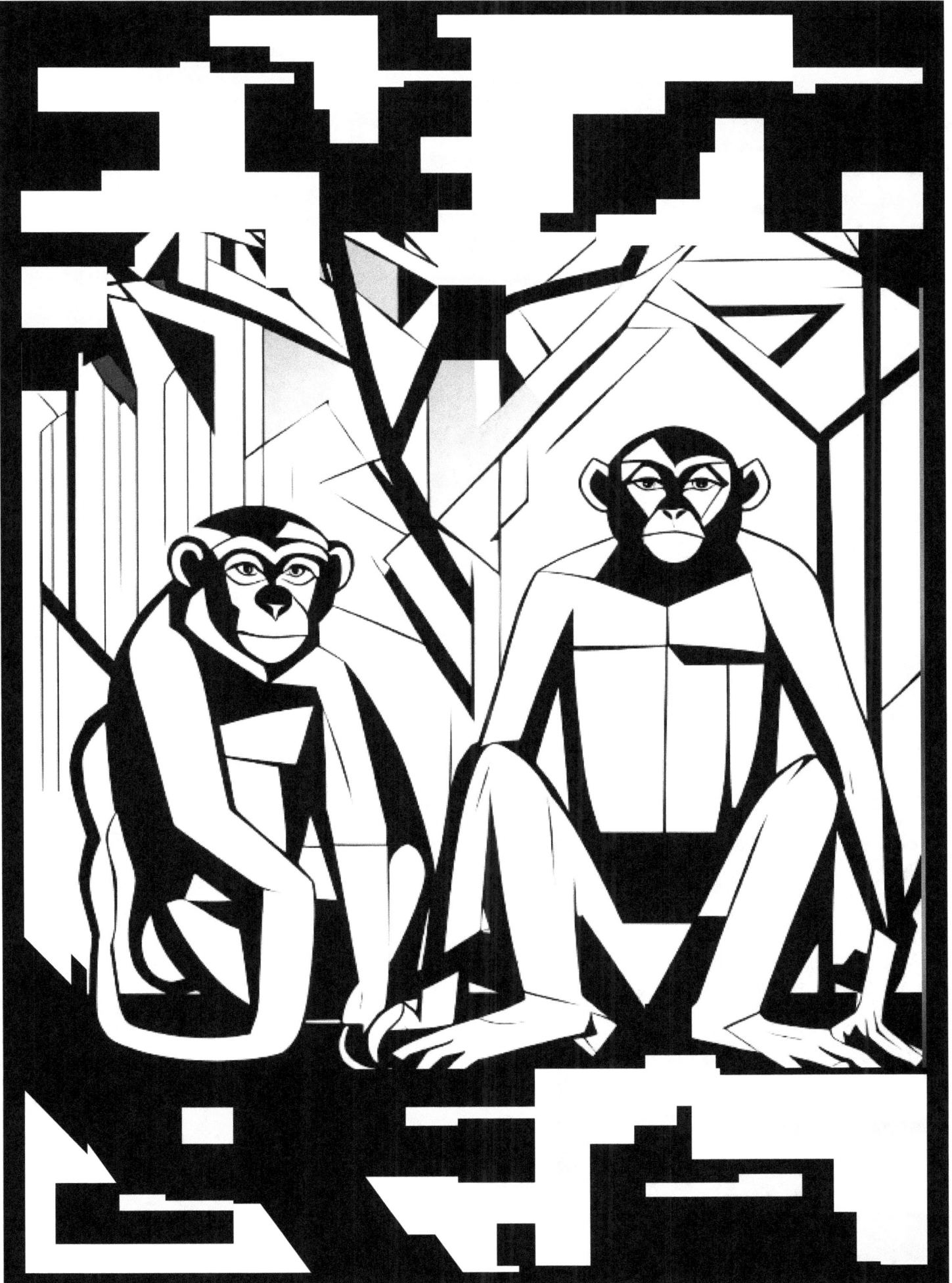

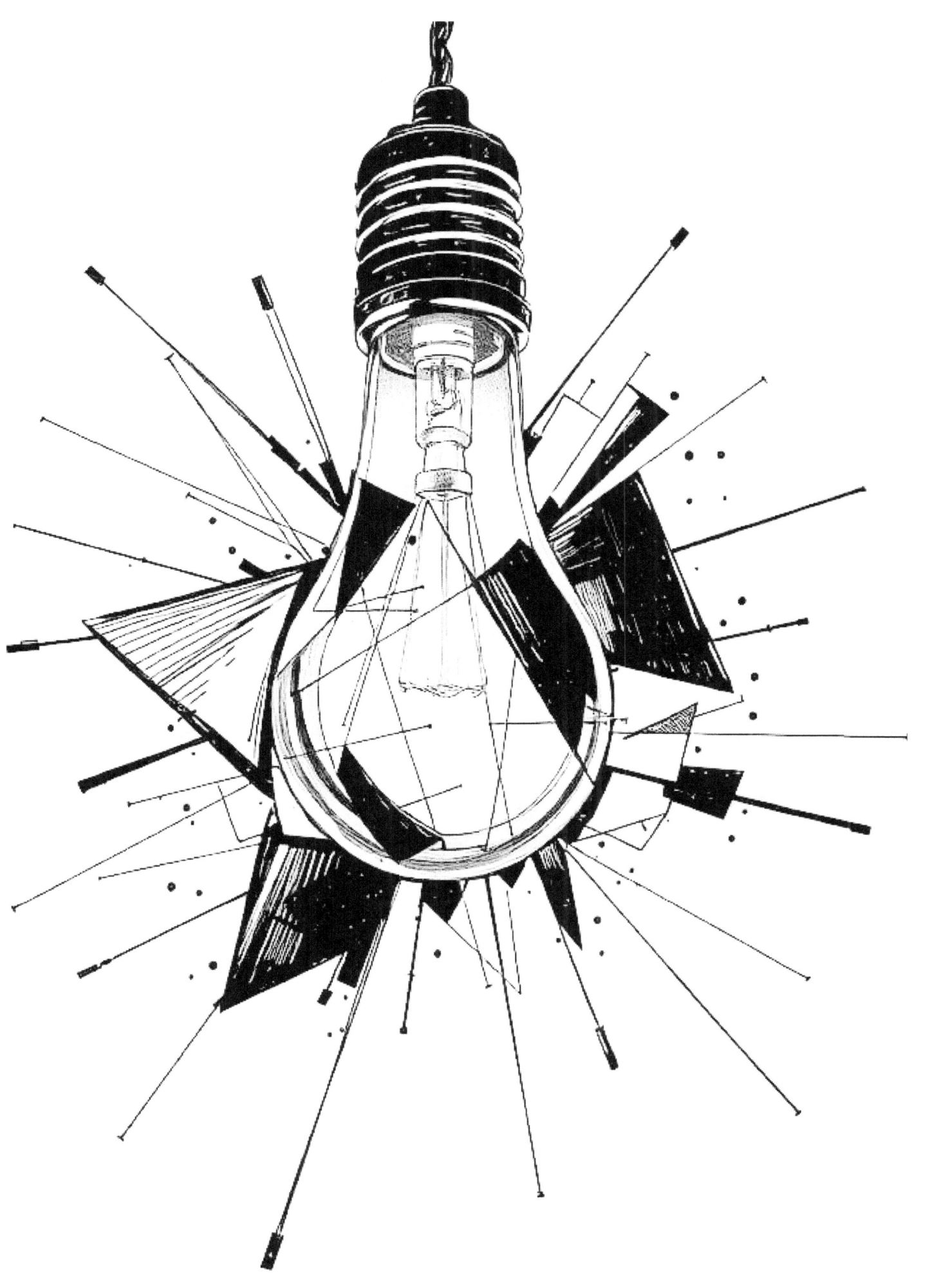

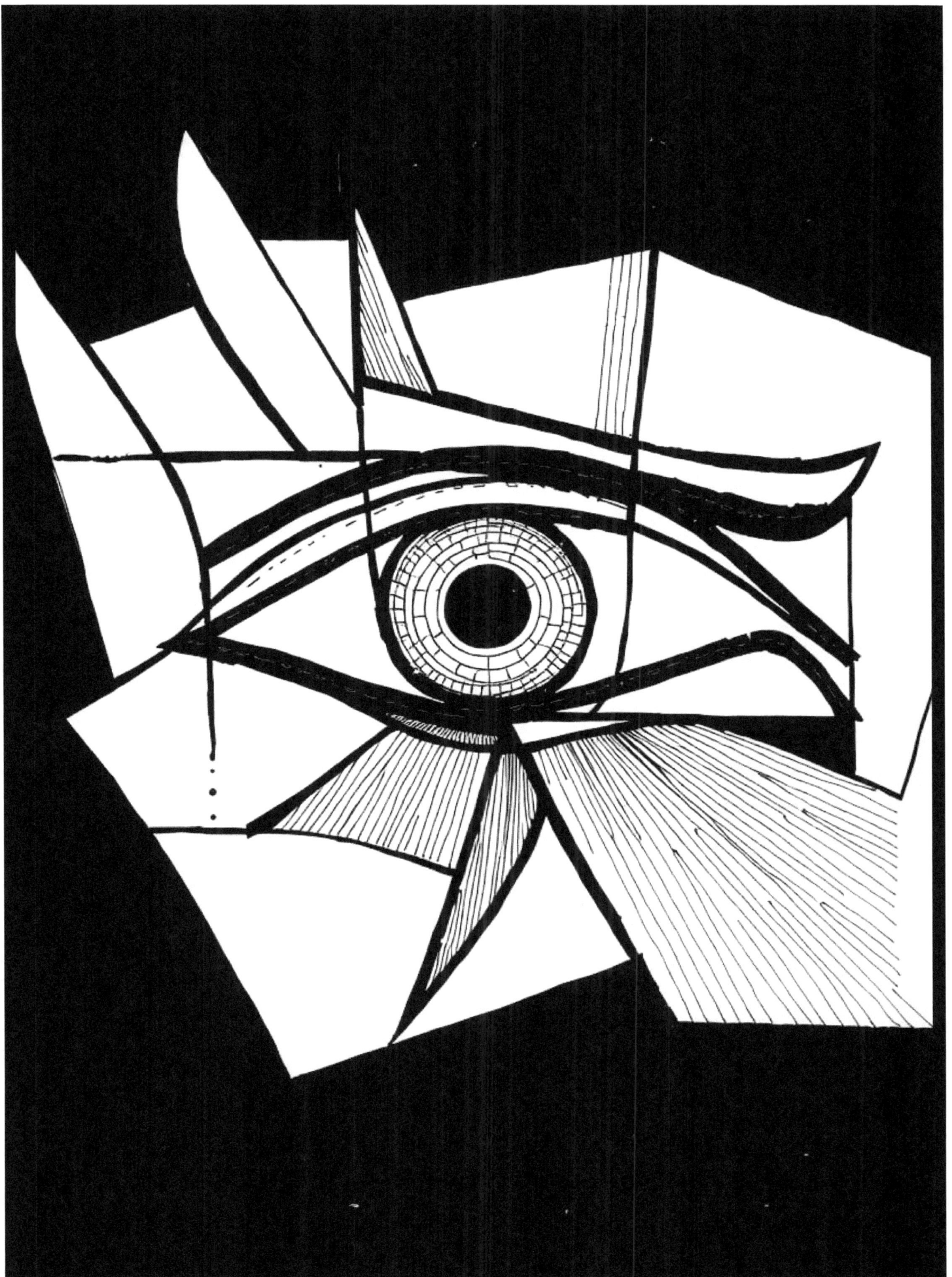

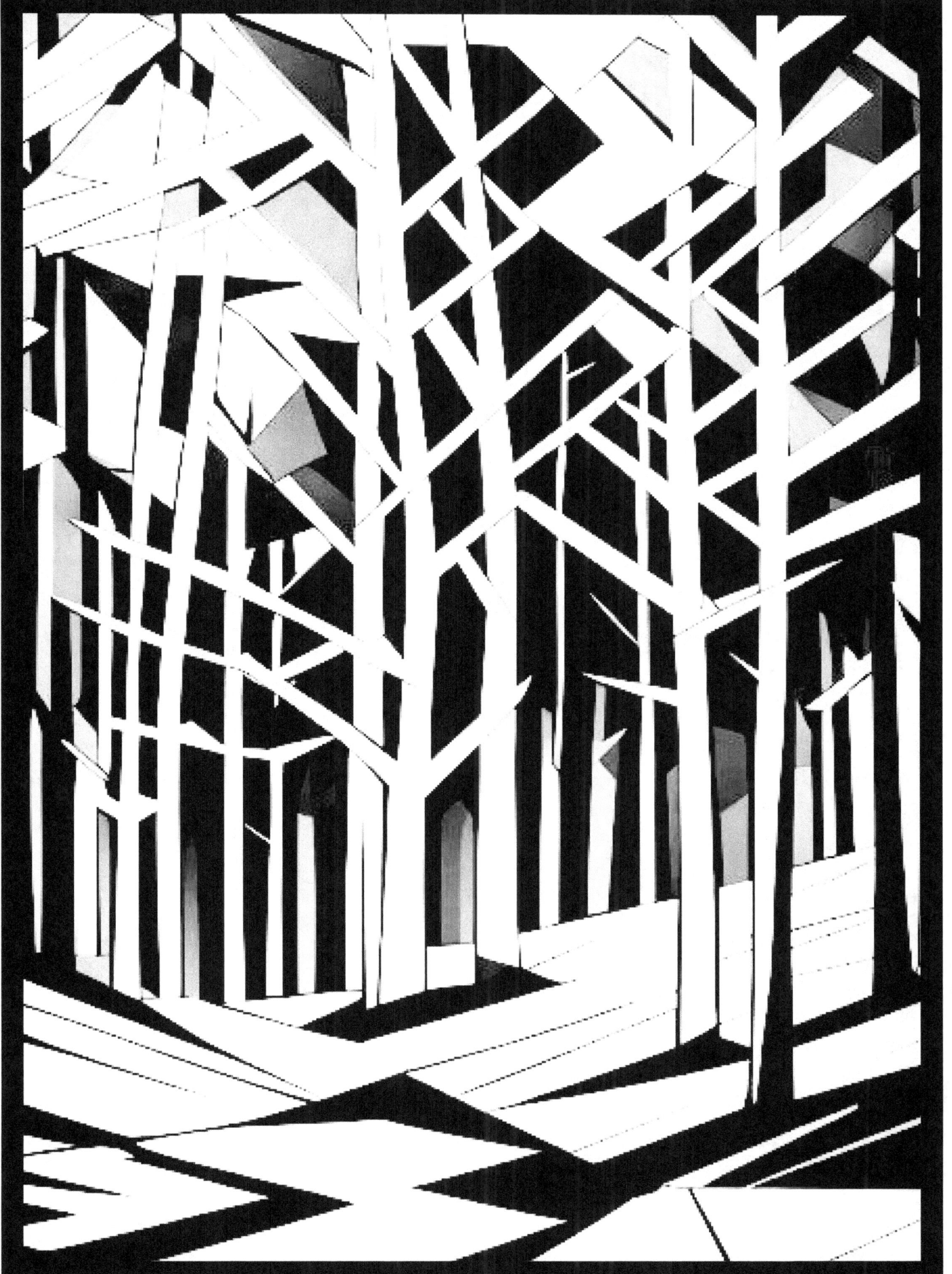

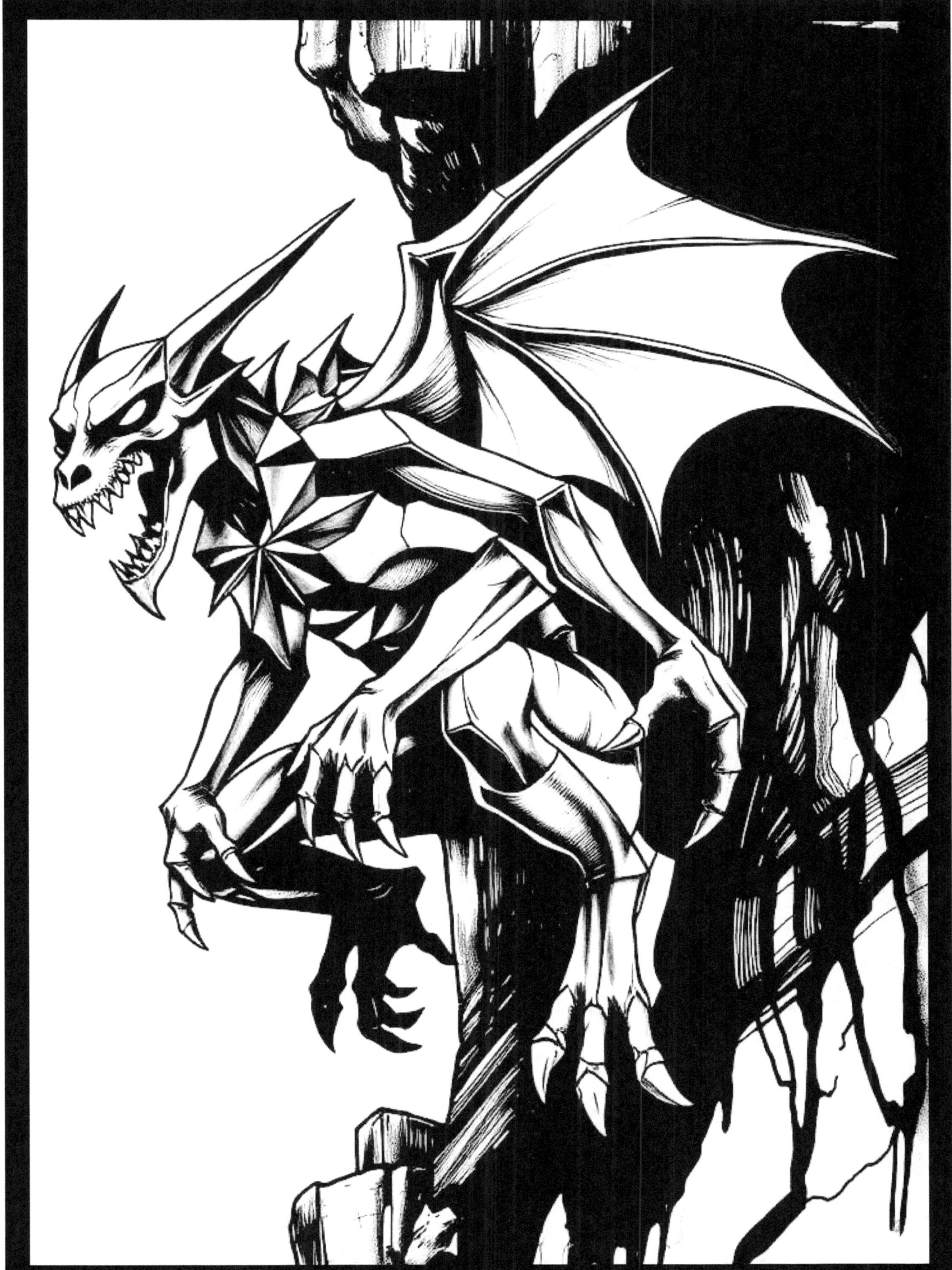

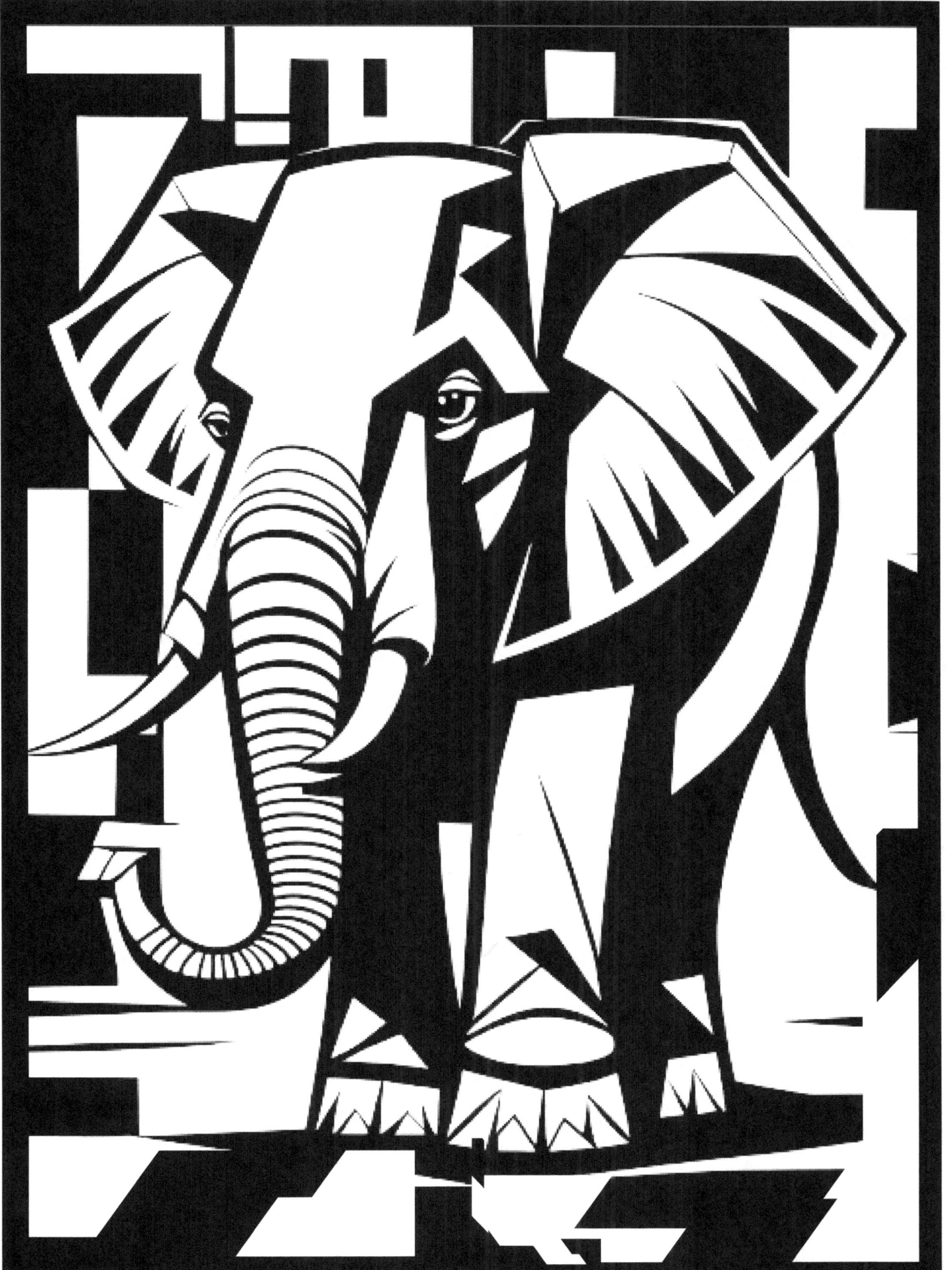

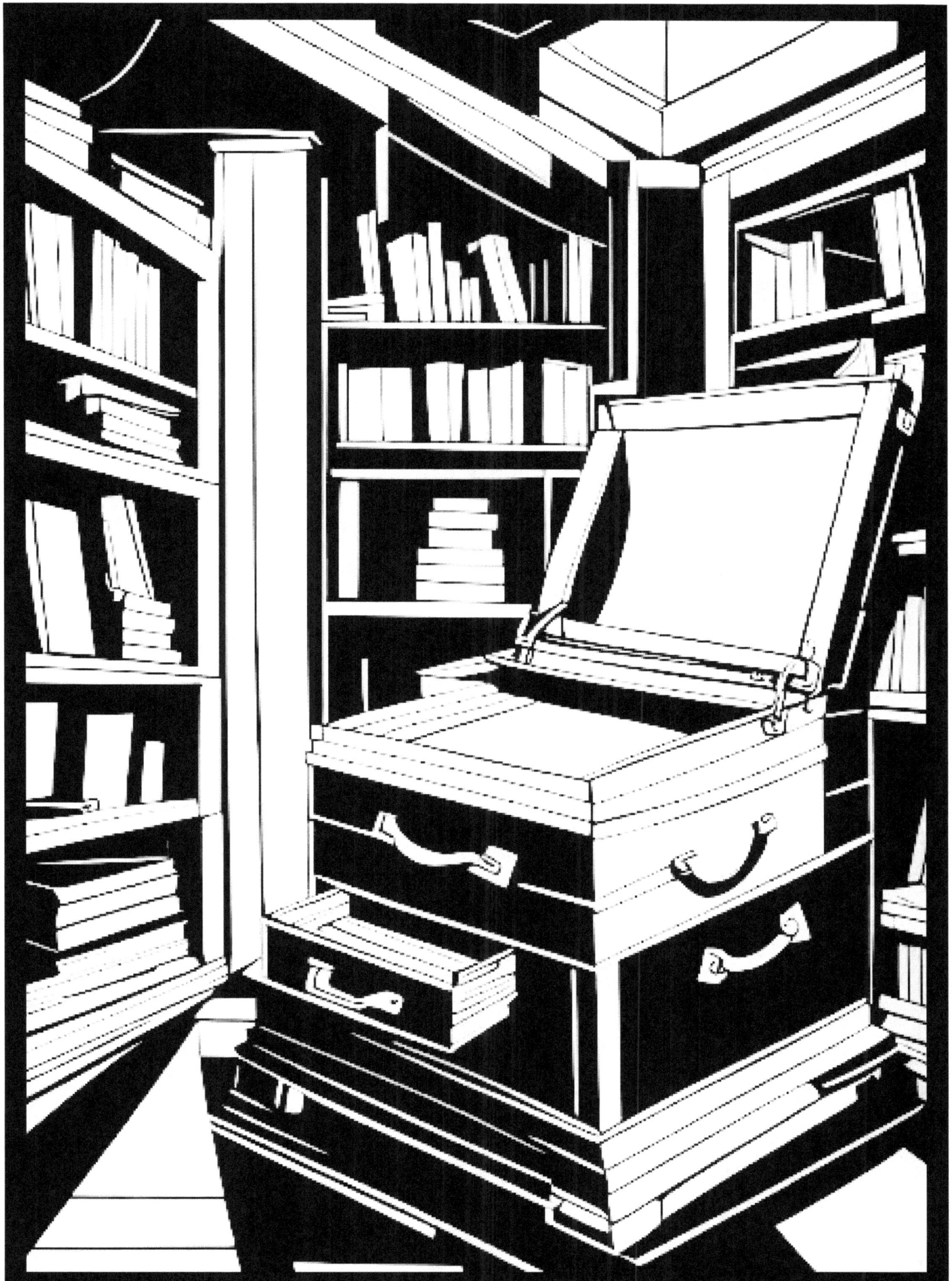

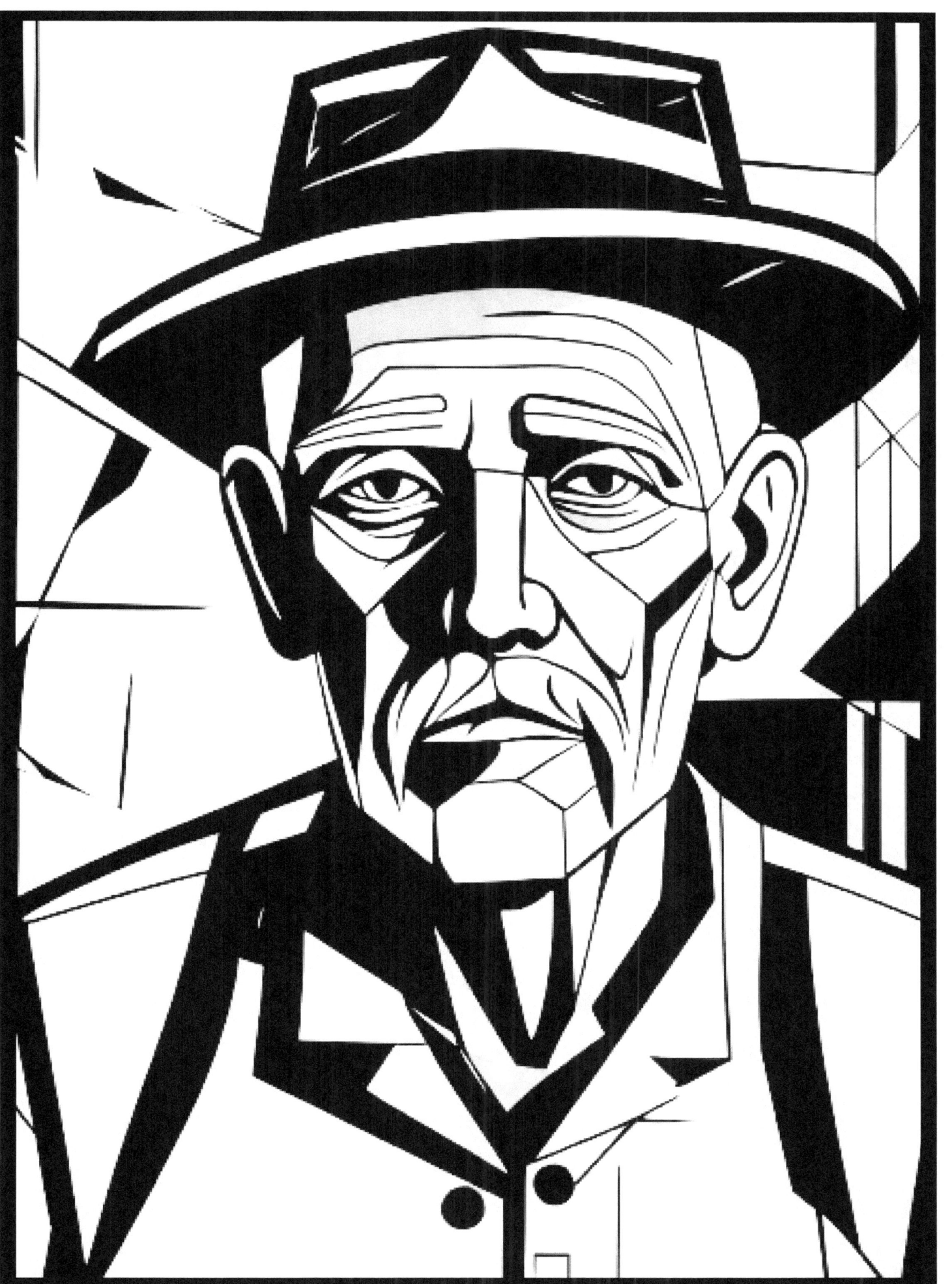

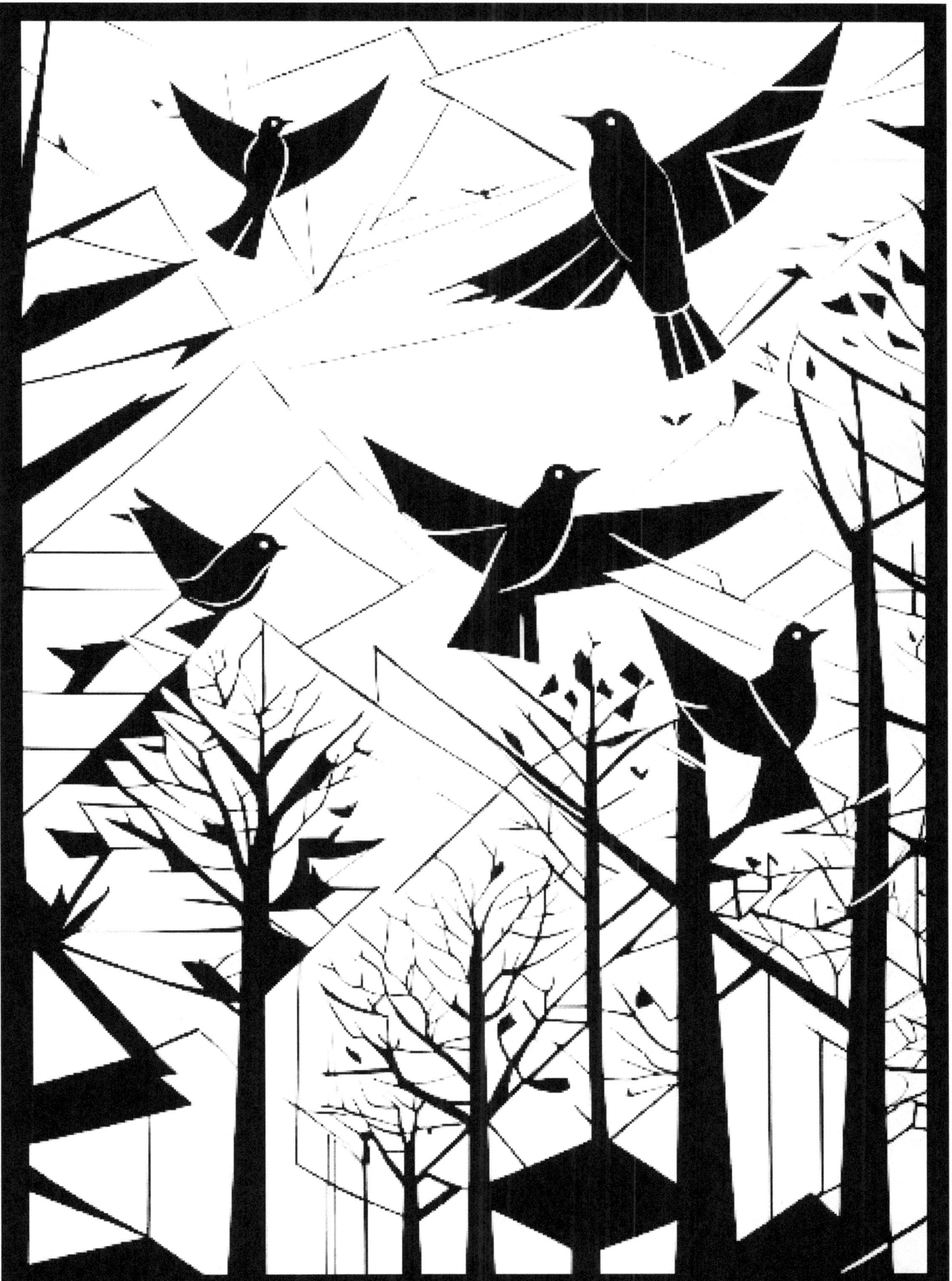

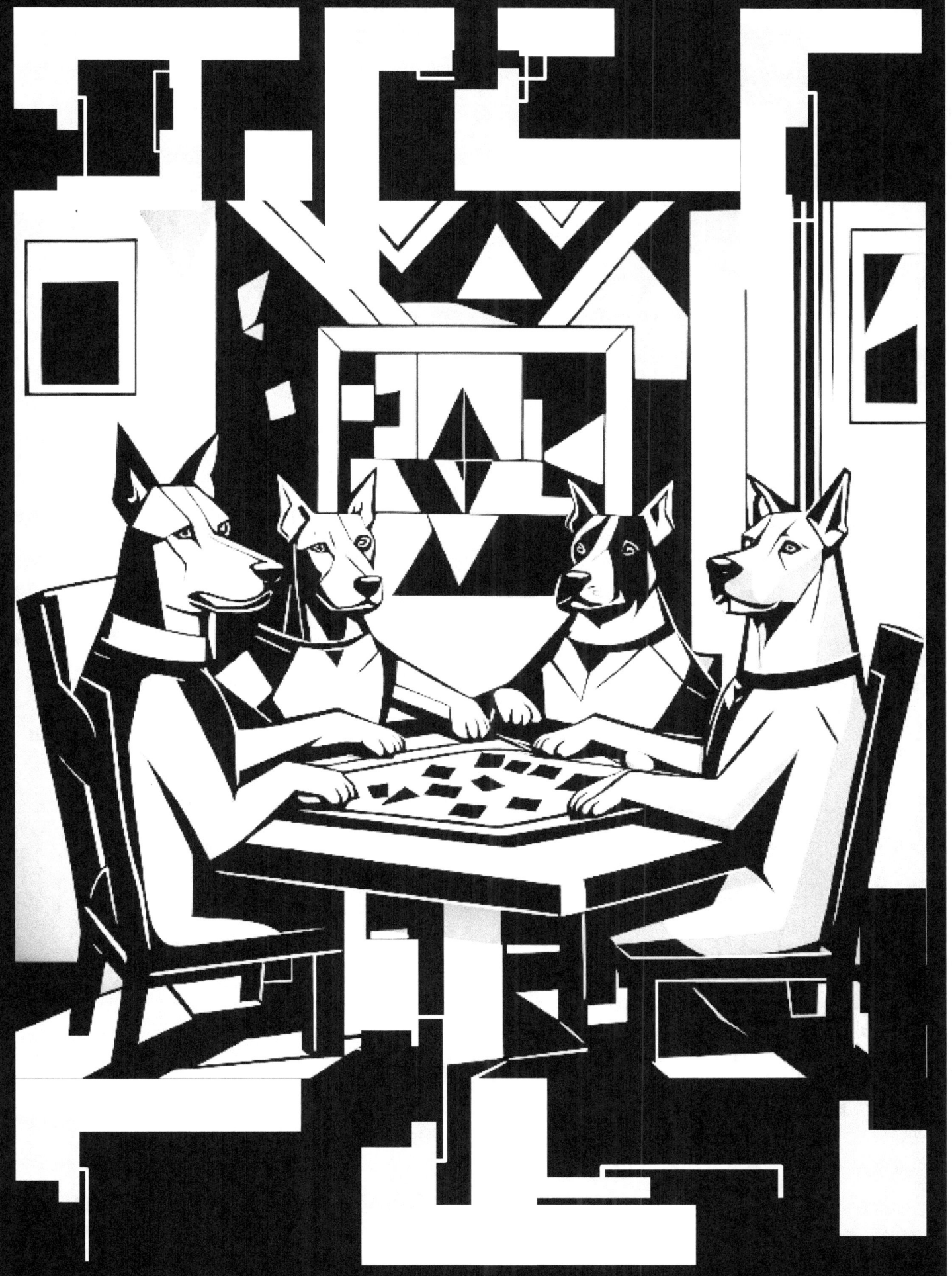

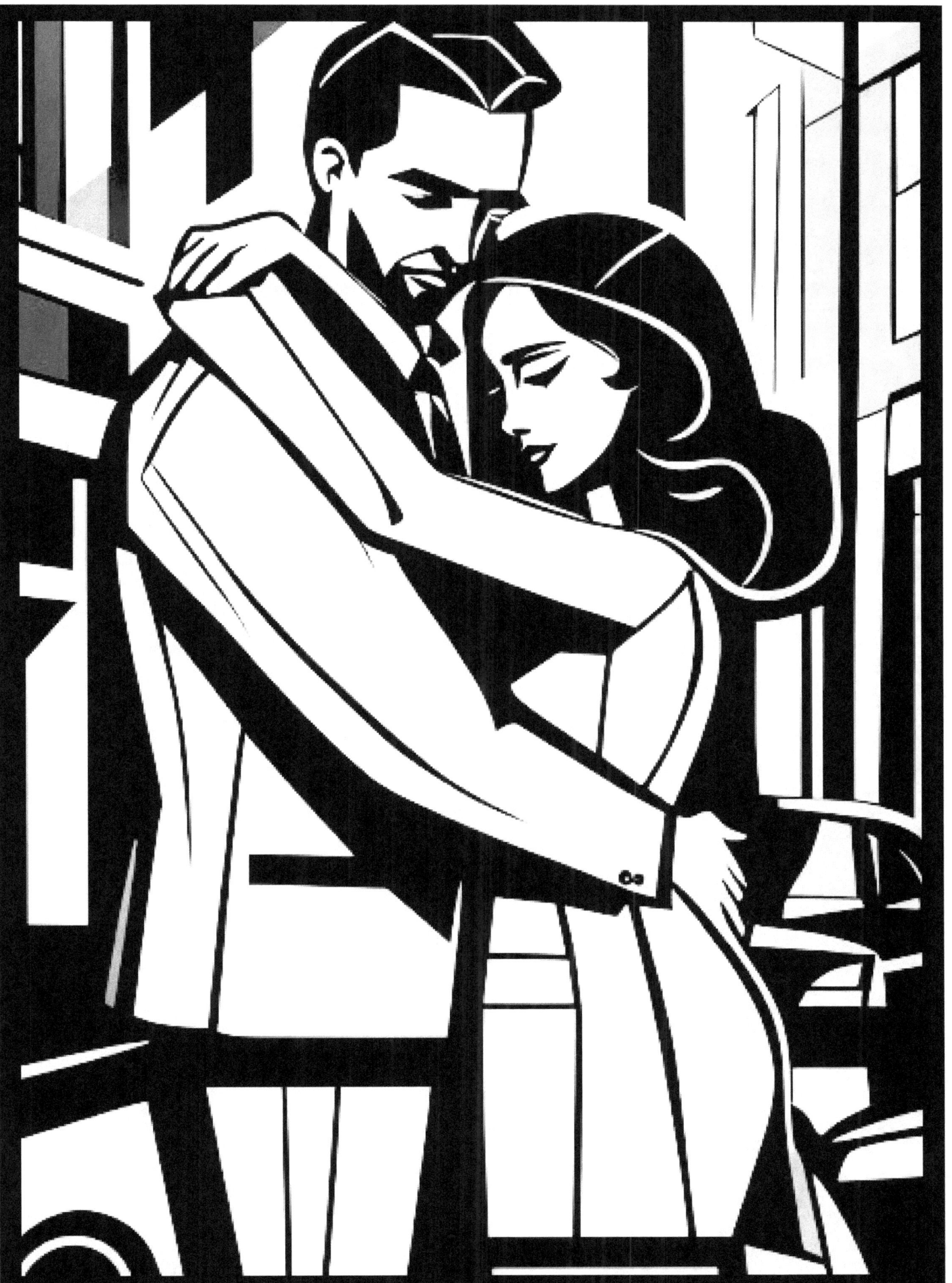

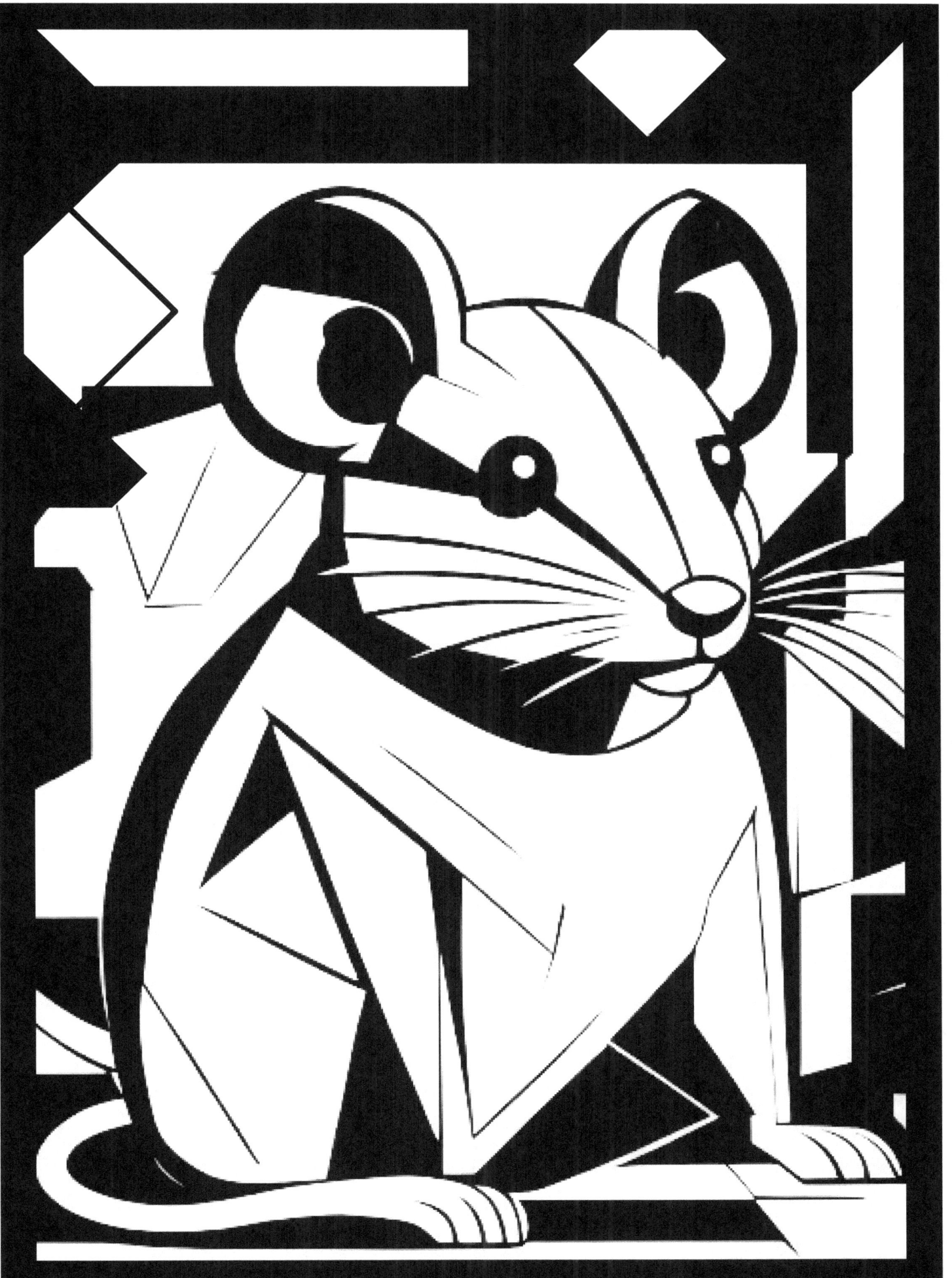

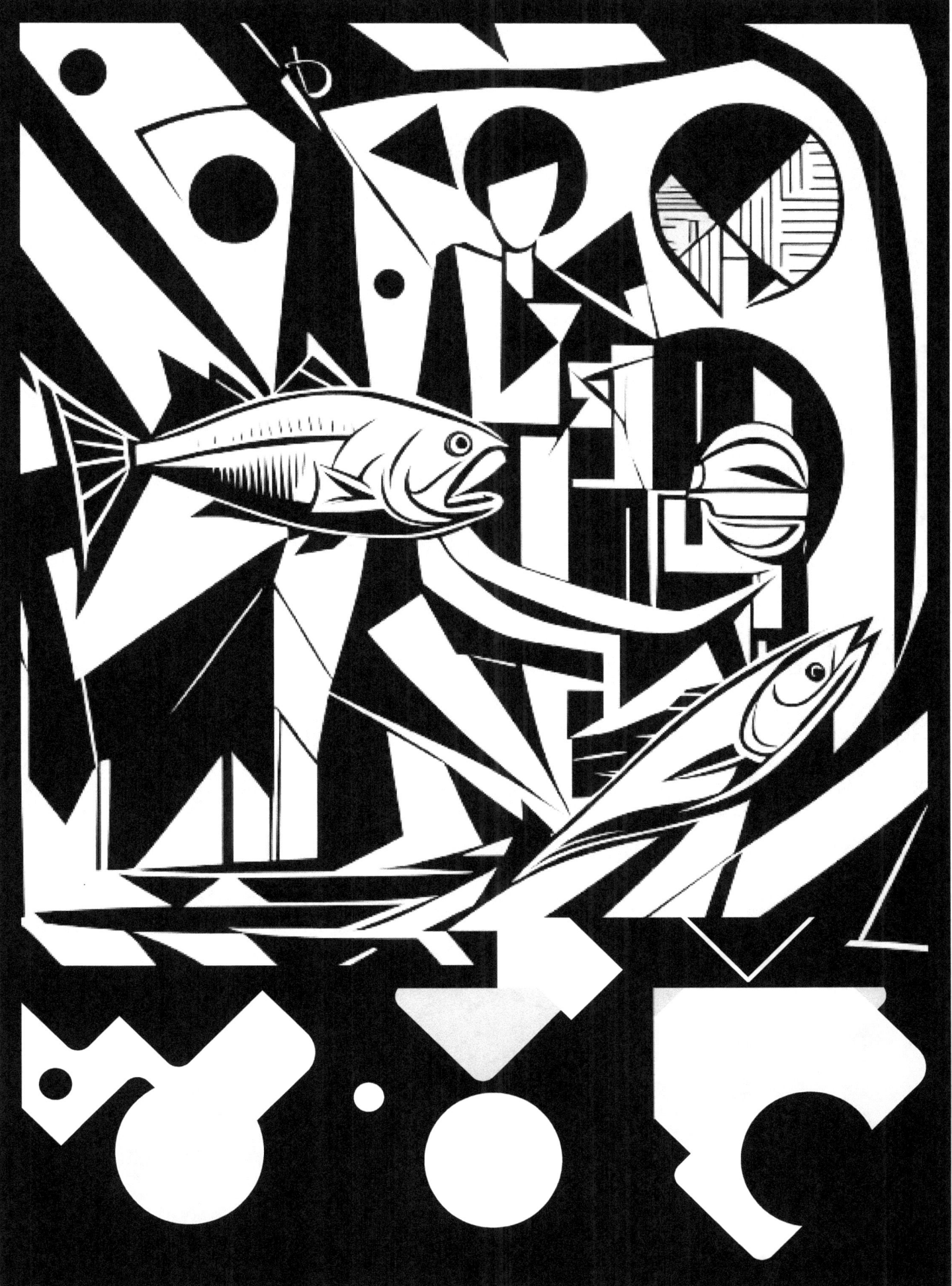

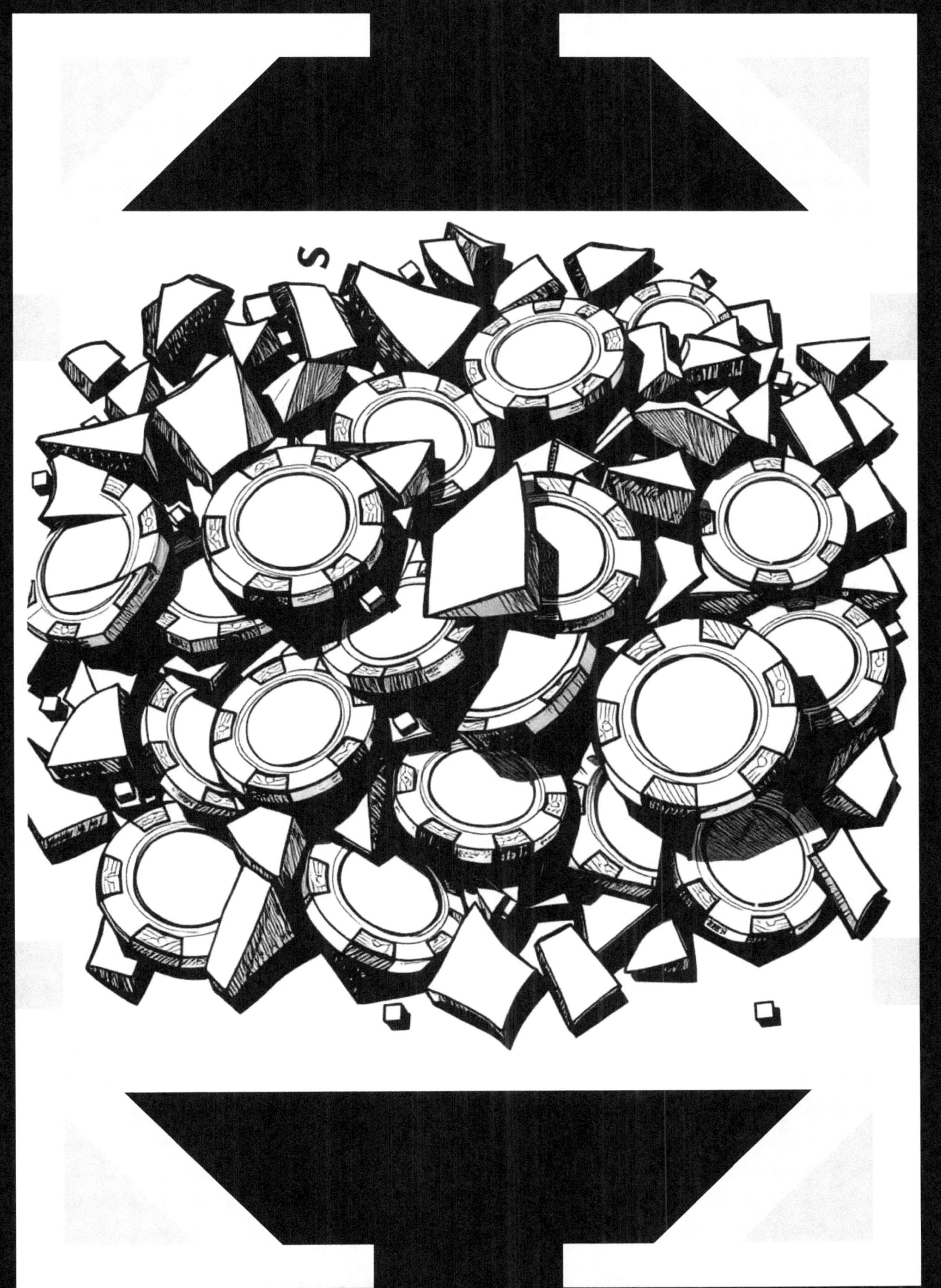

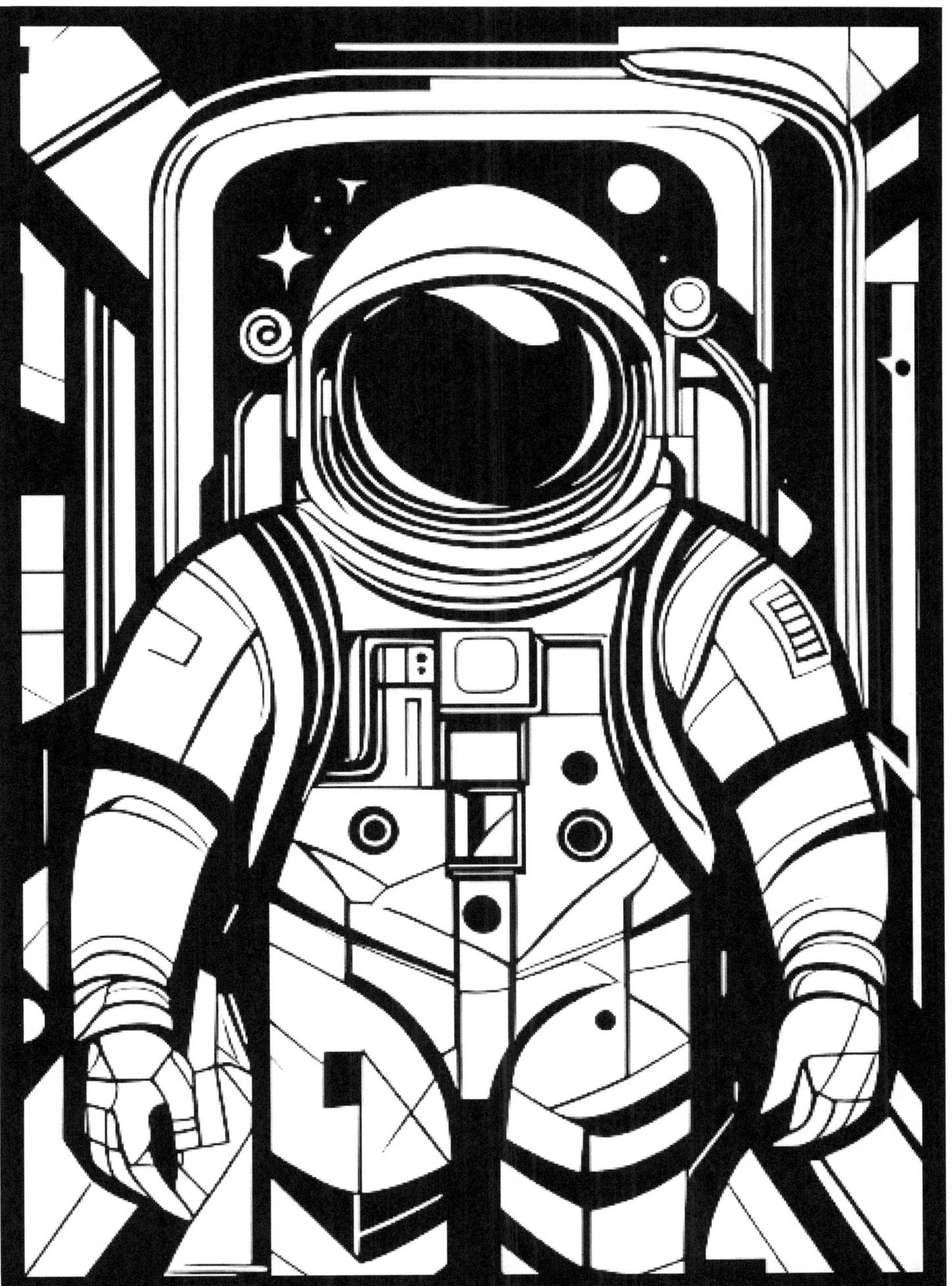

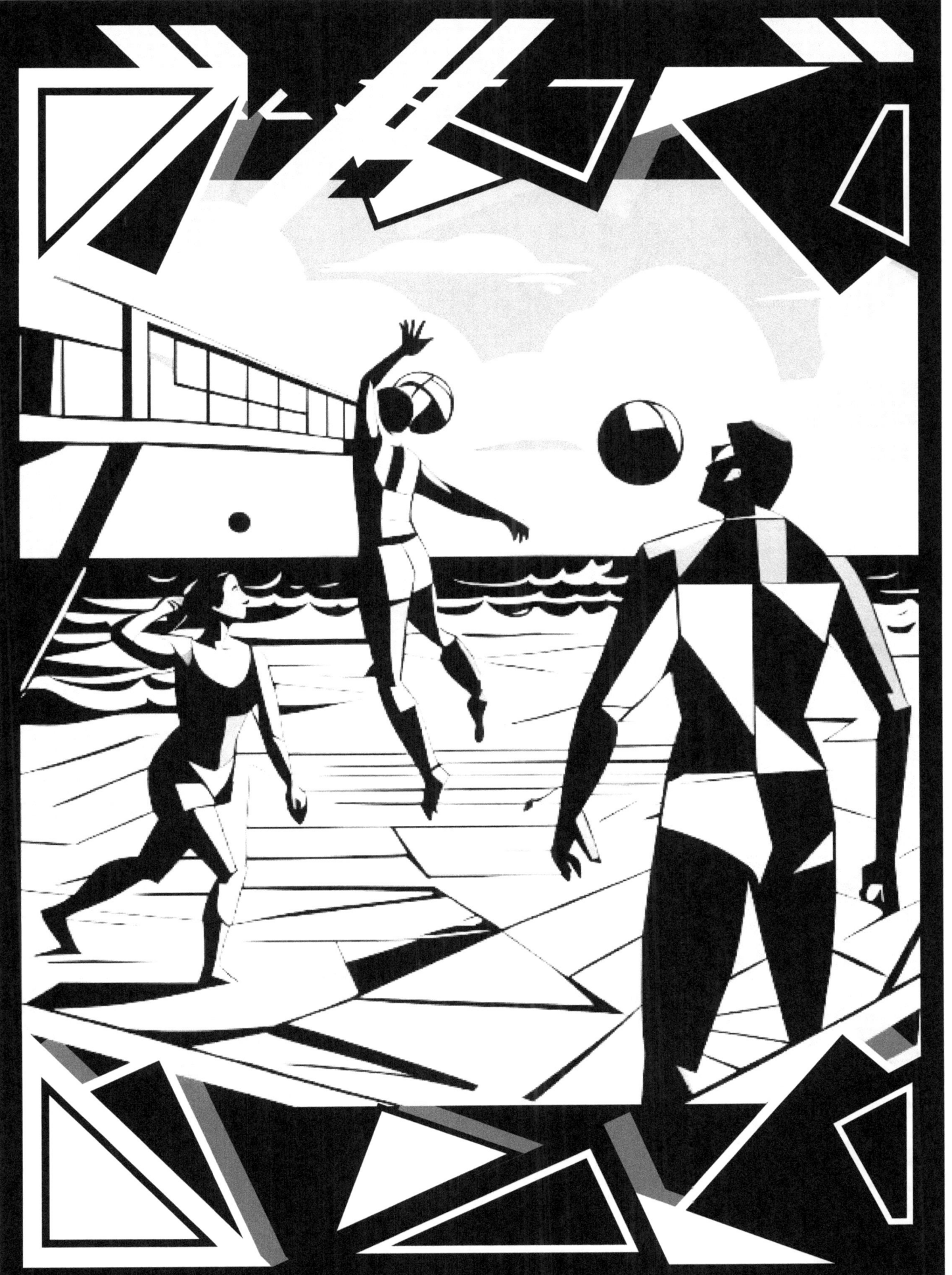

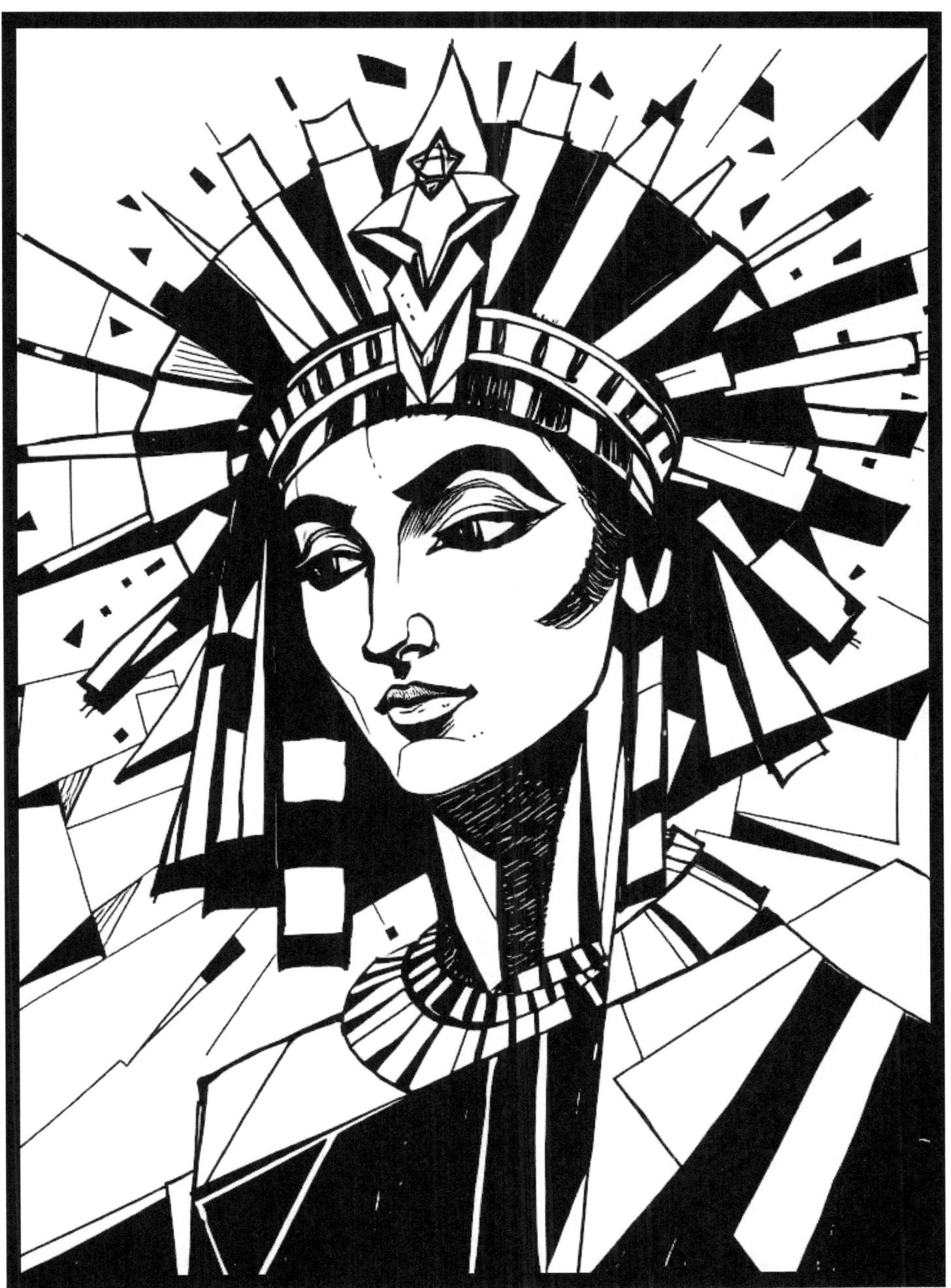

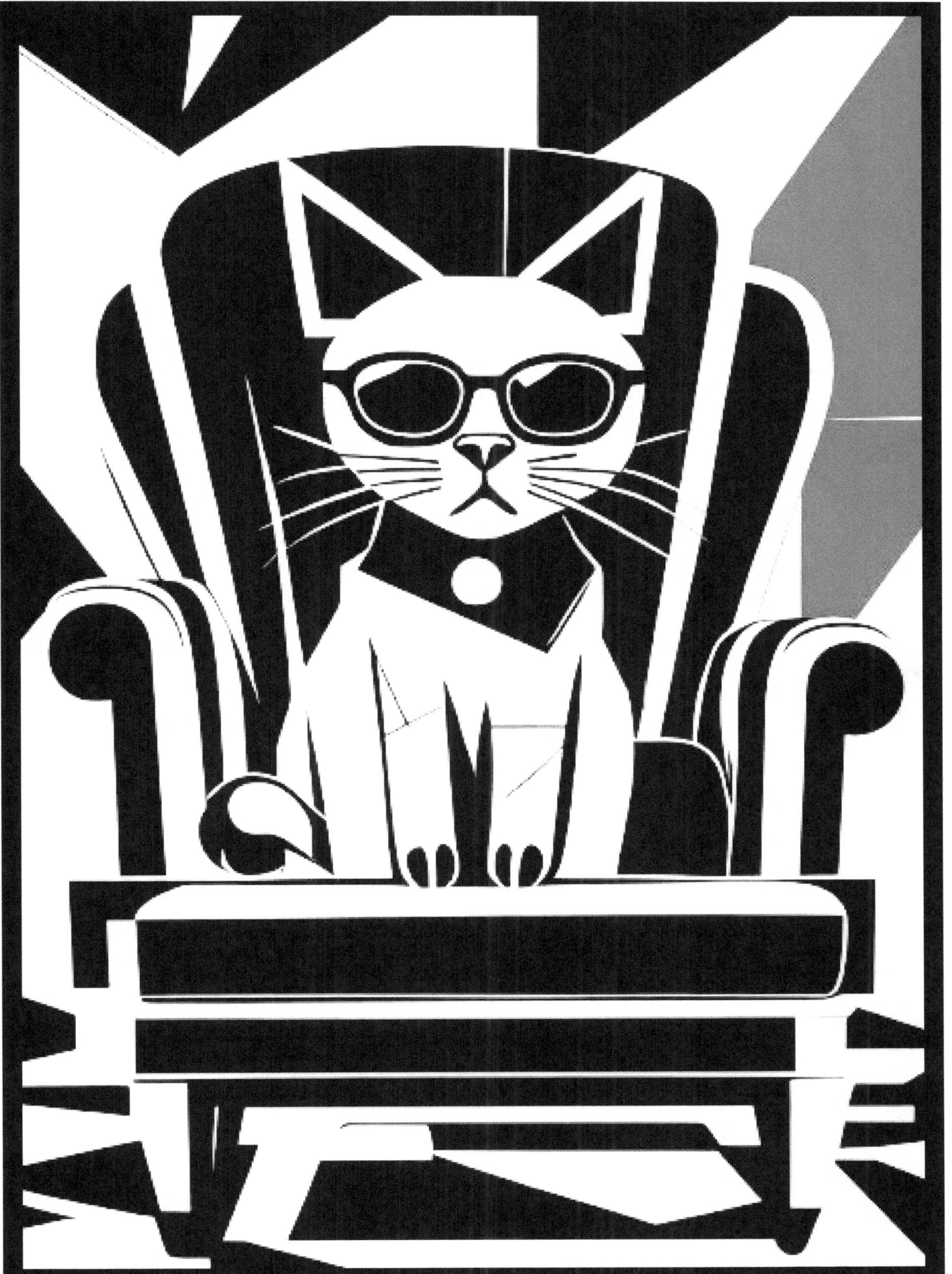

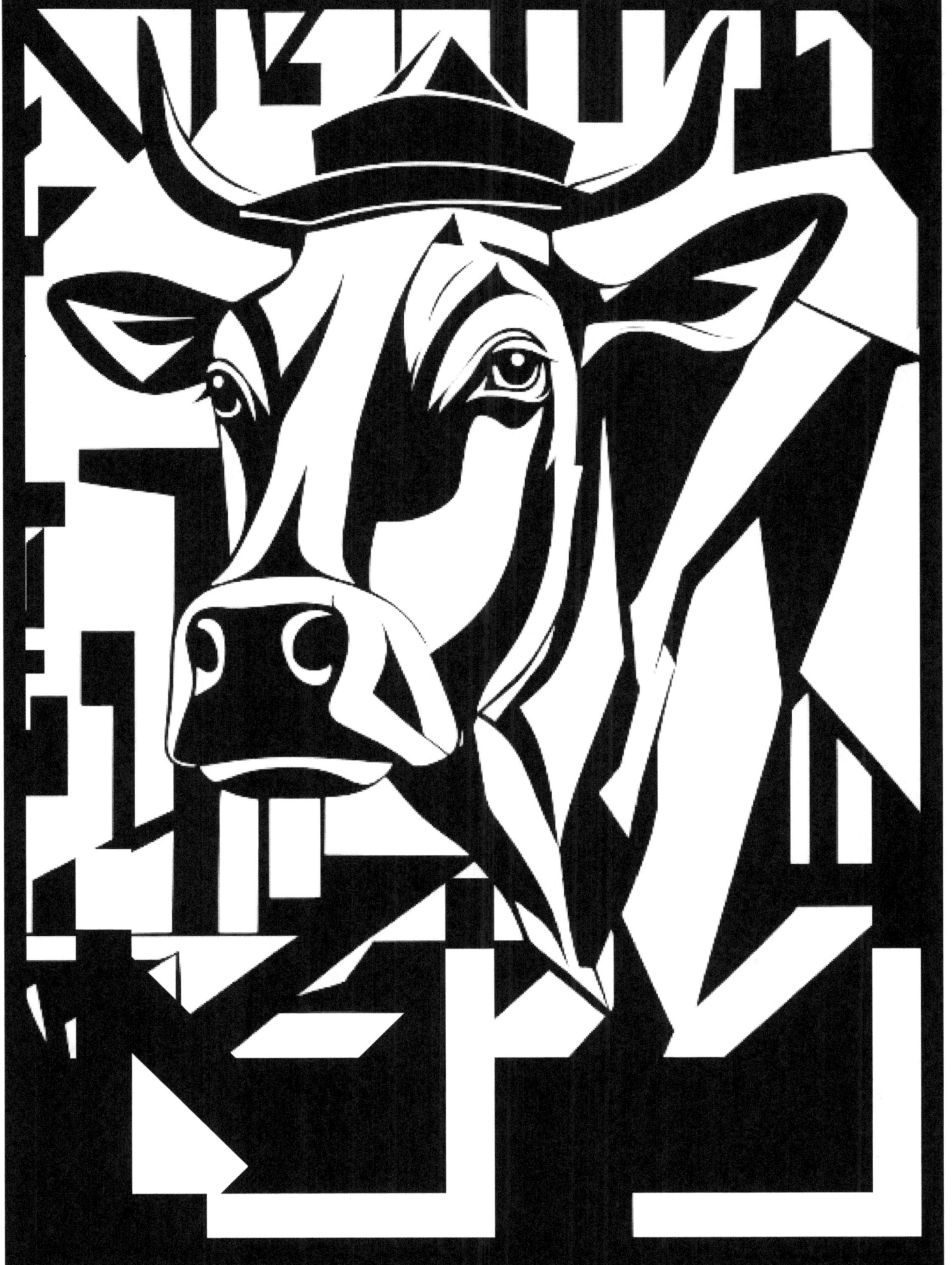

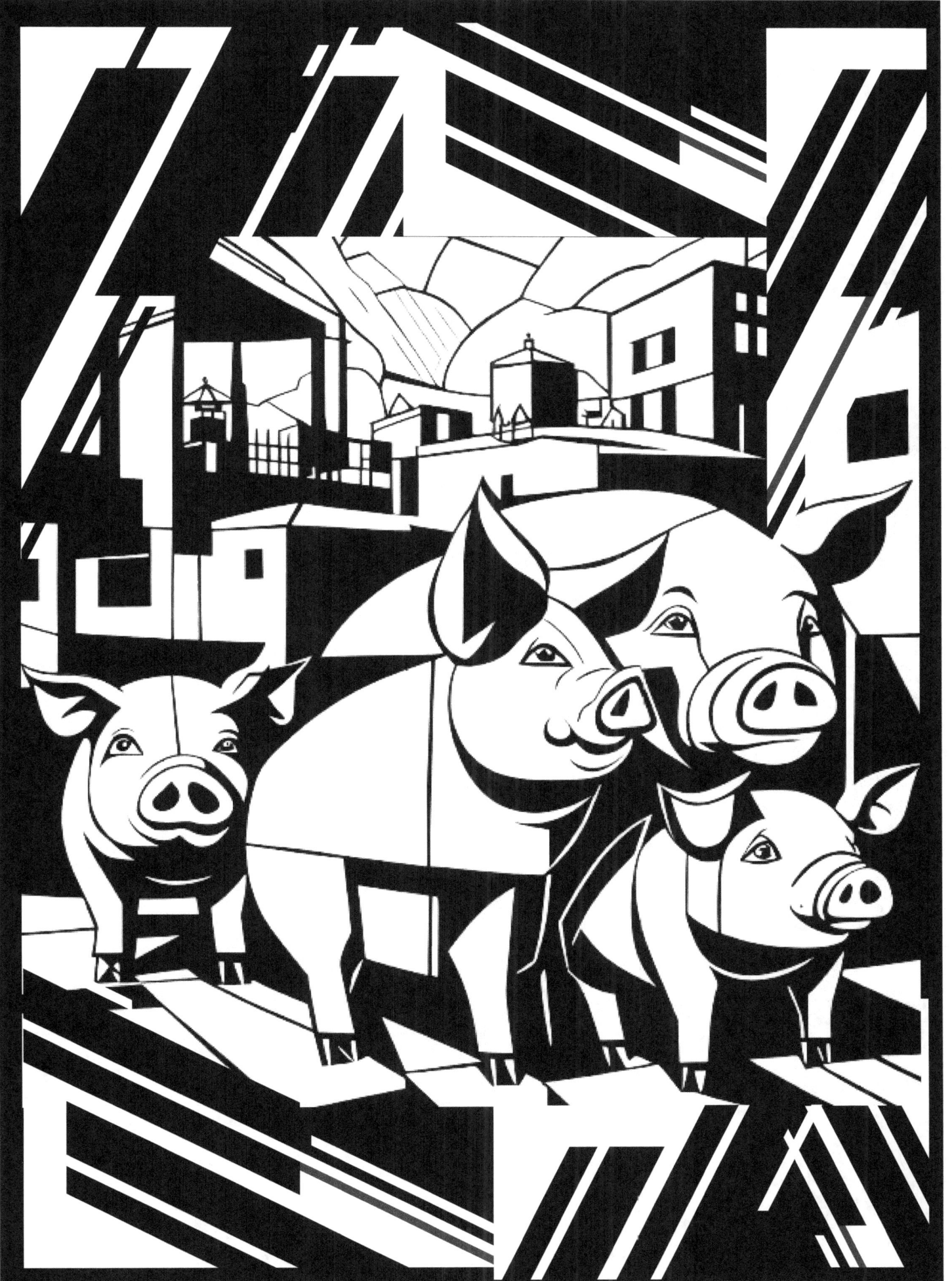

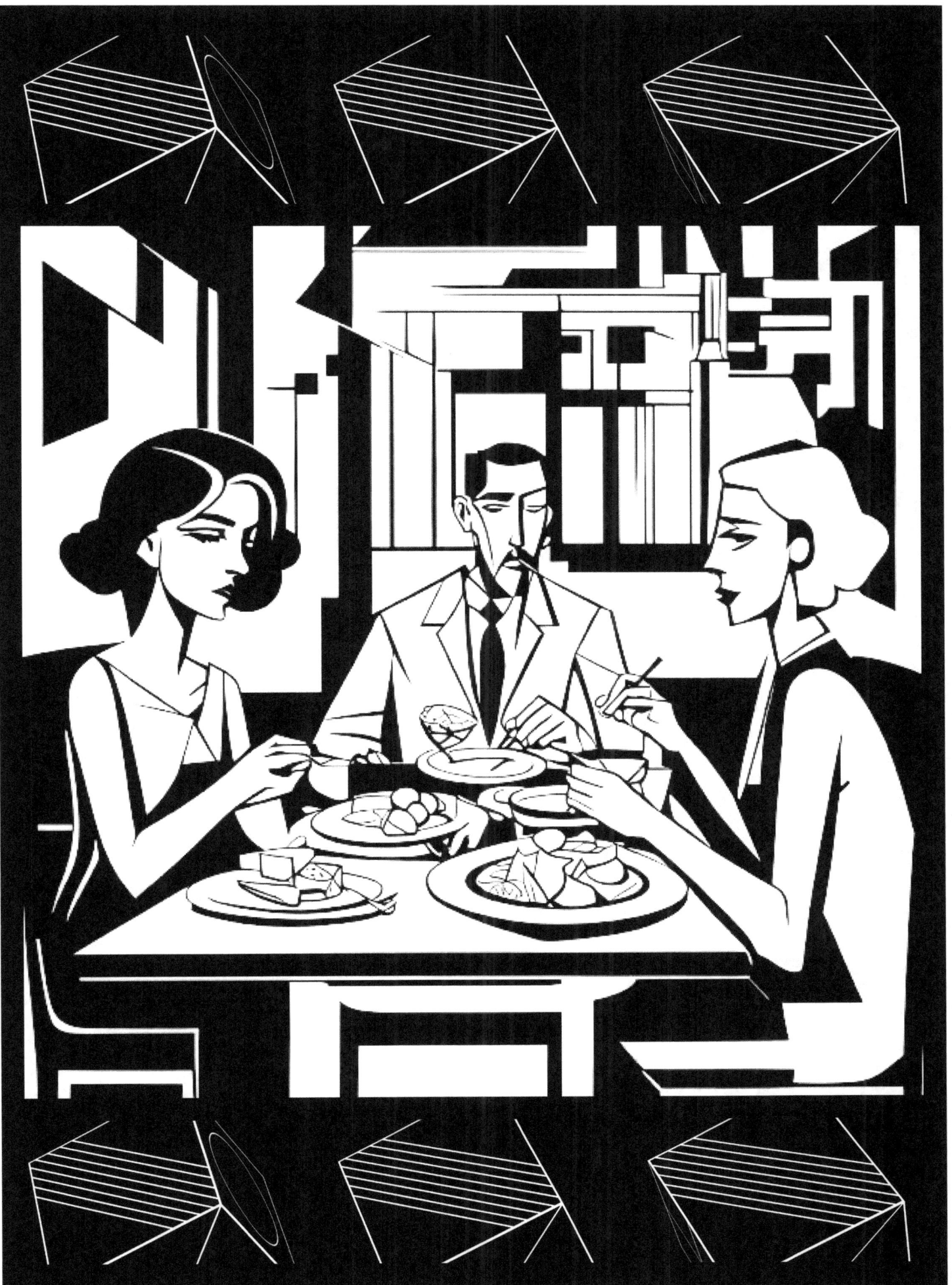

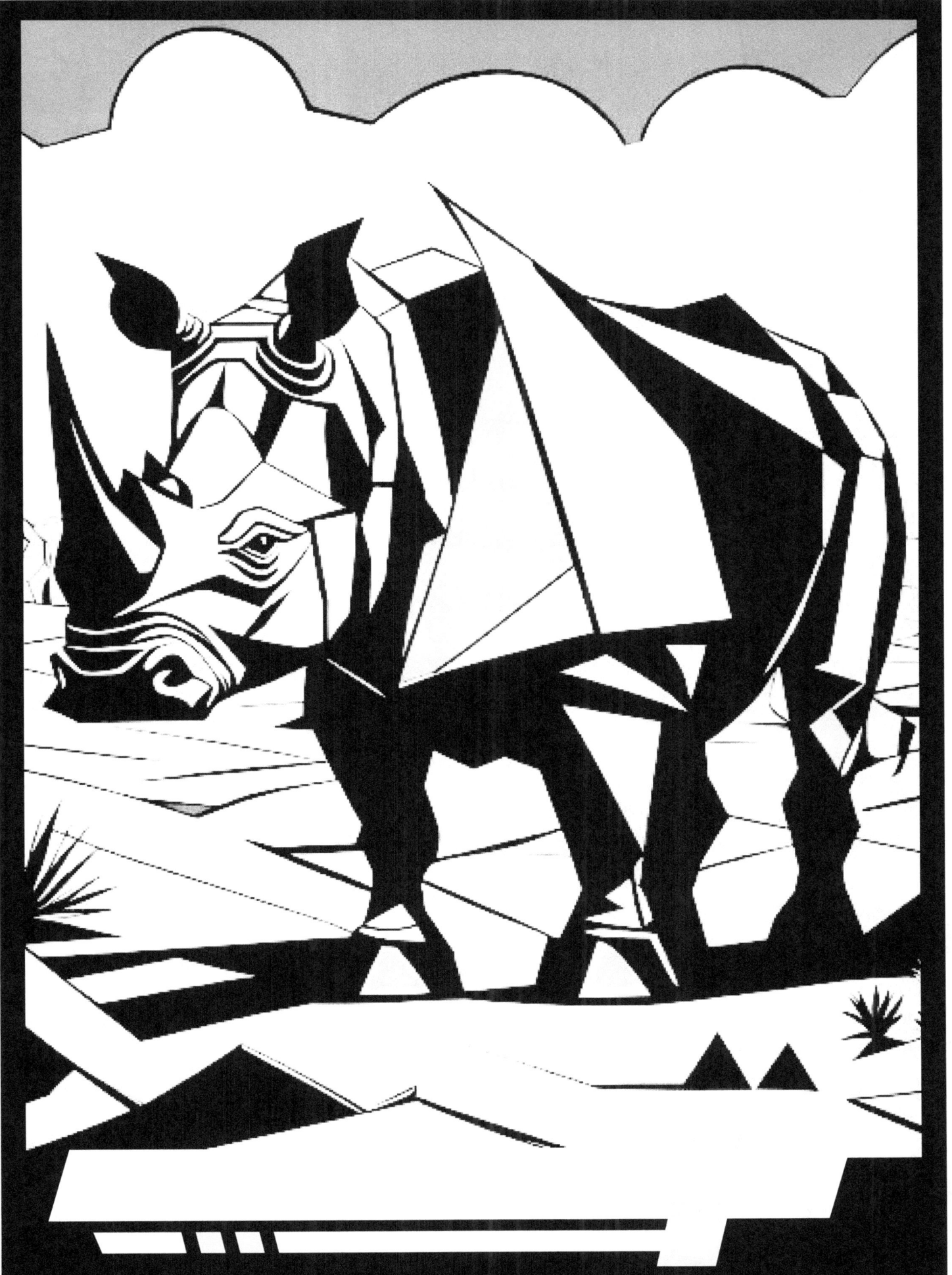

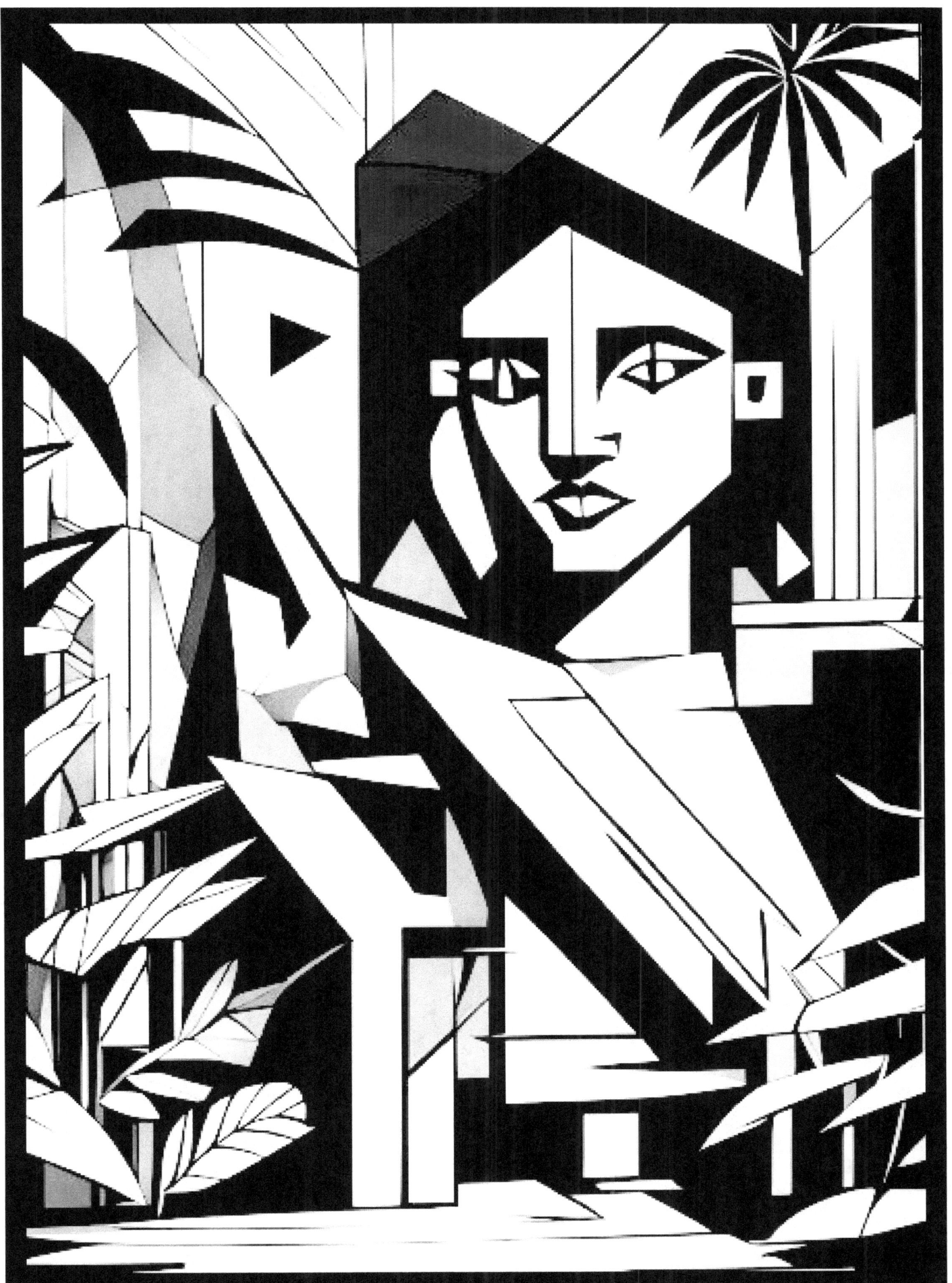

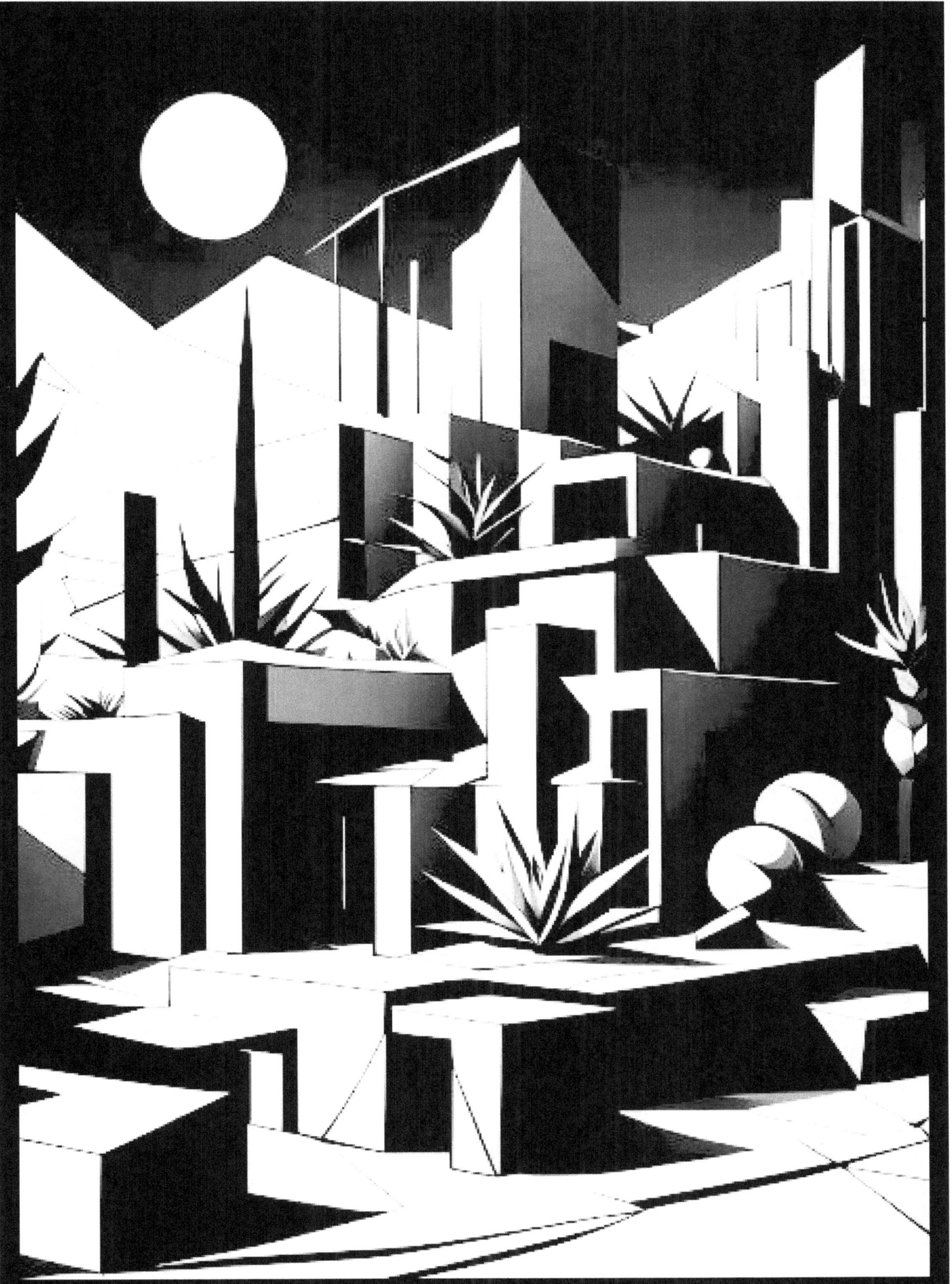

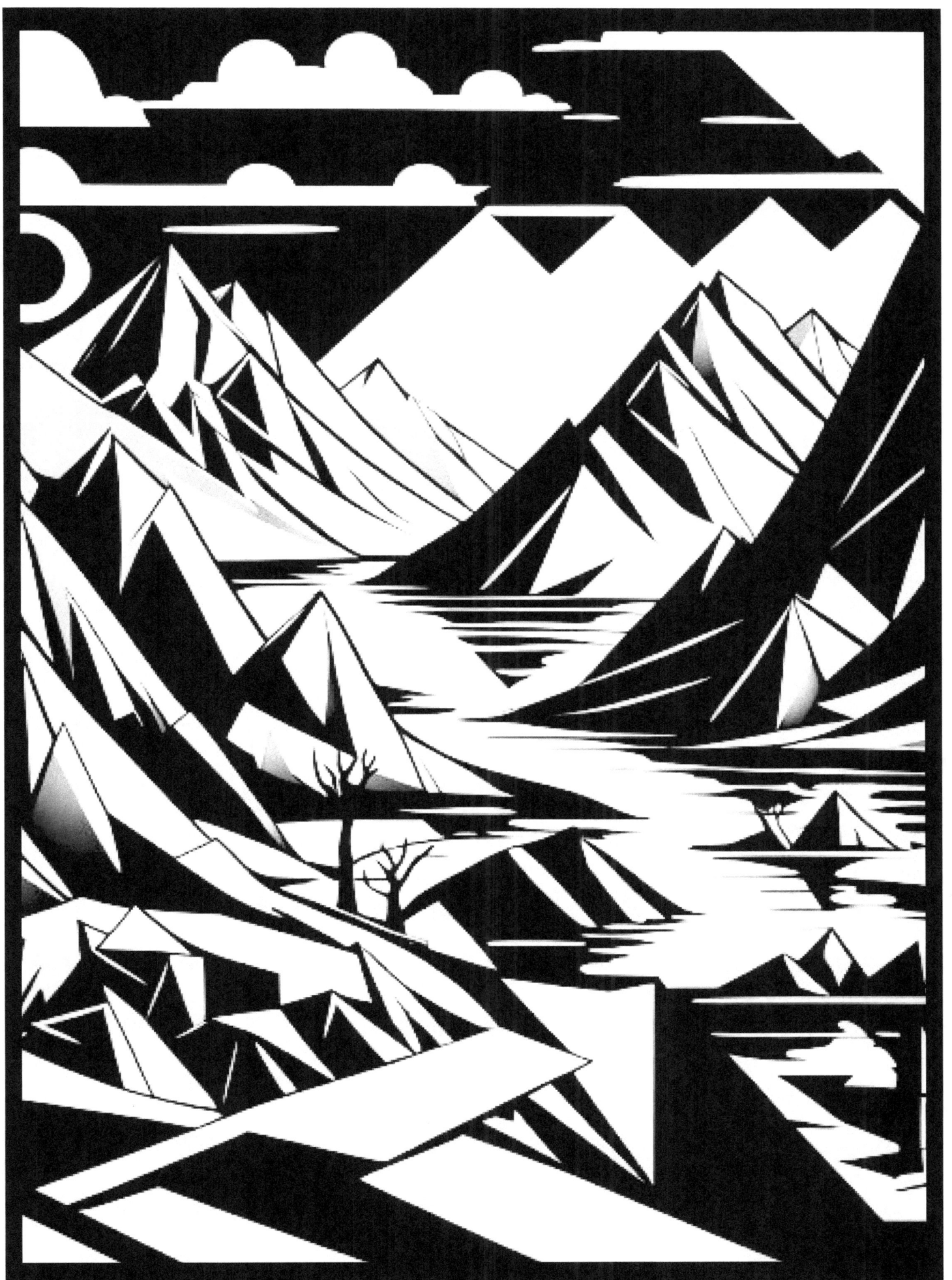

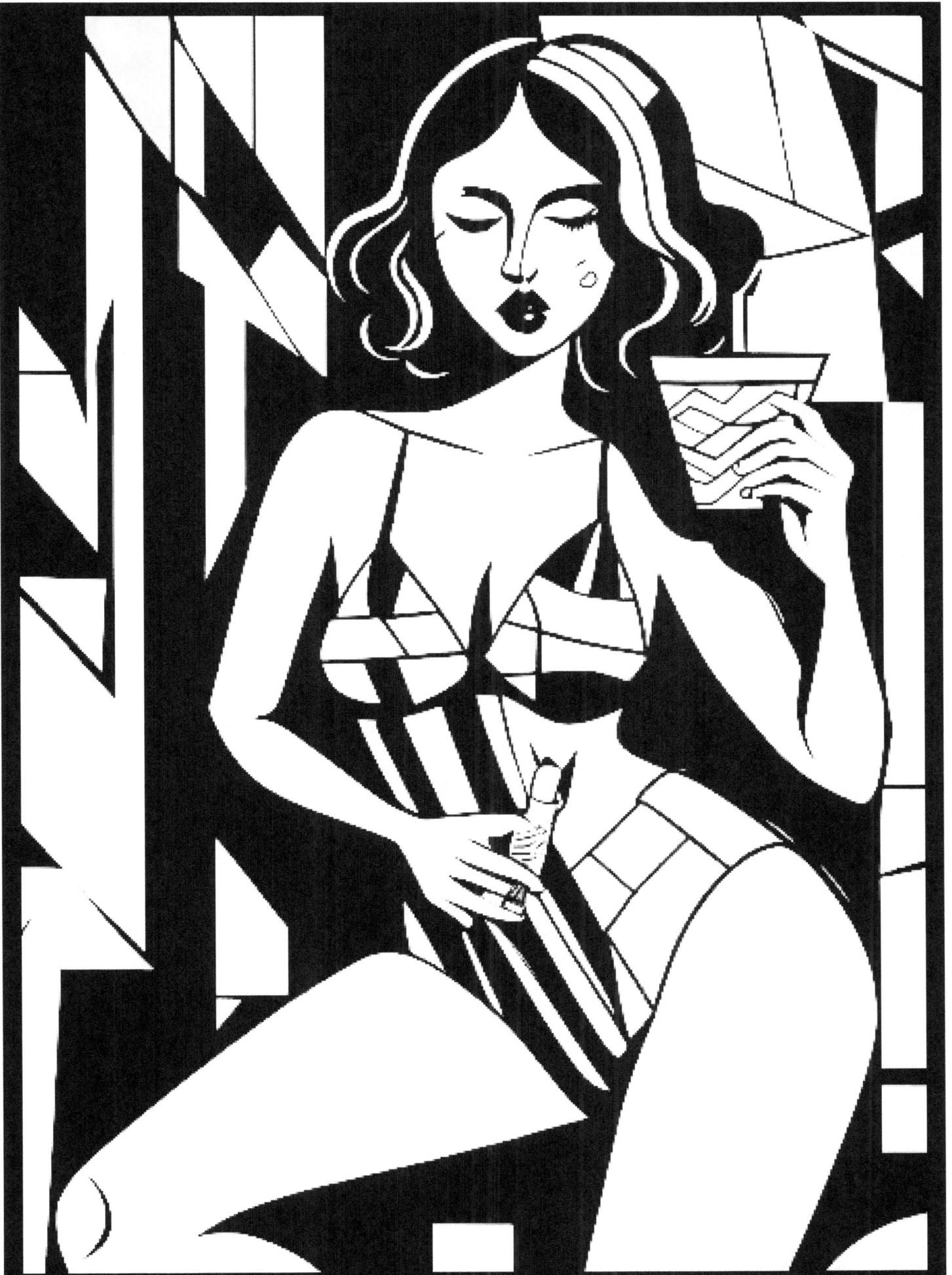

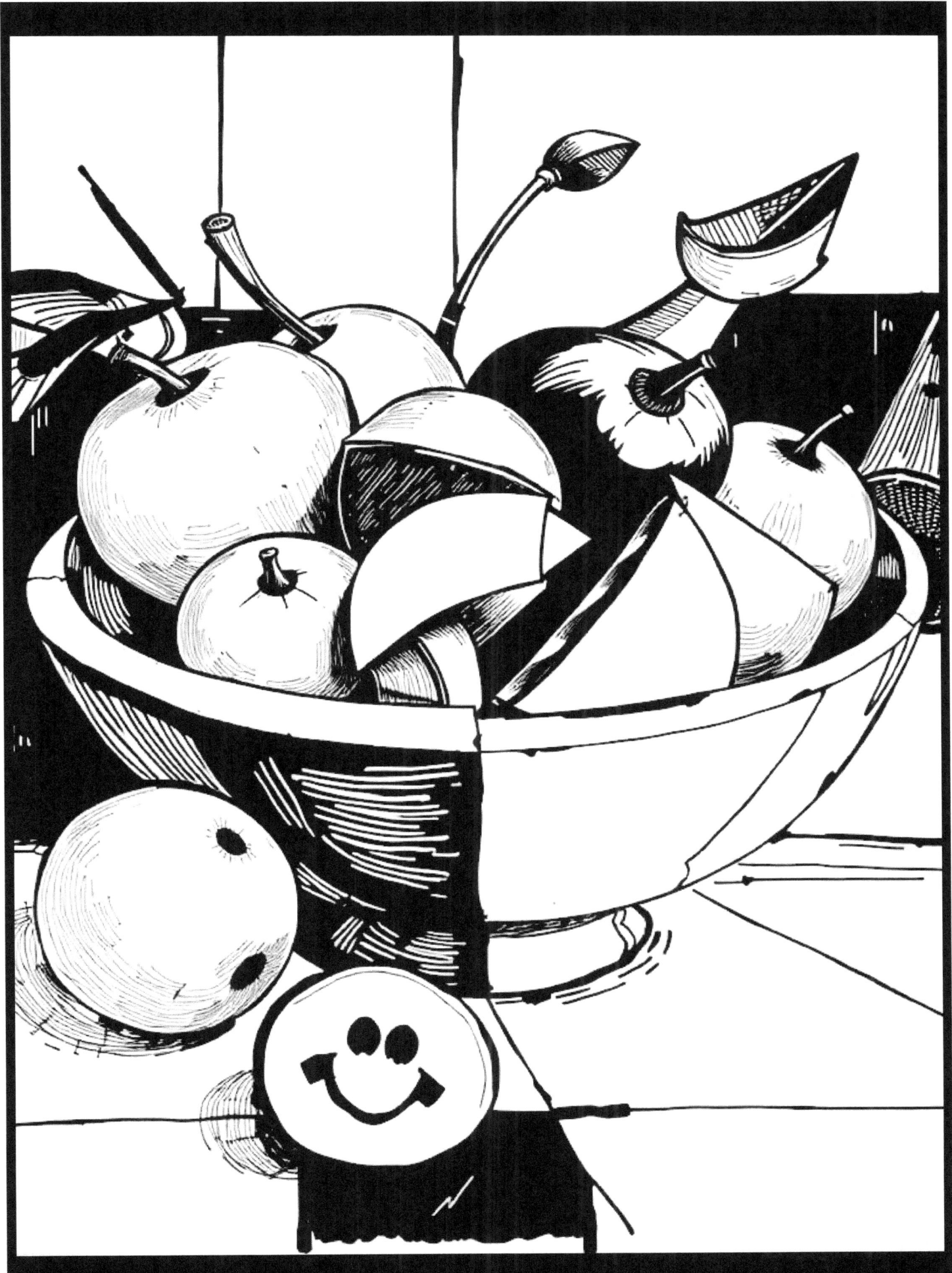